LETTERS
PLAY!

LETTERS PLAY!

A Treasury of Words and Wordplay

Richard Whiteley

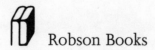

Robson Books

First published in Great Britain in 1995 by Robson Books Ltd,
Bolsover House, 5–6 Clipstone Street, London W1P 8LE

British Library Cataloguing in Publication Data
A catalogue record for this title is available from the British Library

Book design by Harold King

ISBN 0 86051 992 9

Typeset in 11/13pt Joanna by Columns Design and Production Services Ltd, Reading
Printed by Butler & Tanner Ltd, London and Frome

Introduction

Words – where would we be without them?

Well, we'd be grunting away to each other, I suppose. Just think of what wouldn't exist if there were no words: radio, with just music, no patter of DJs; television with just pictures; newspapers with acres of white space; the House of Commons with rows of honourable members gesticulating and grunting to each other . . . so what's new?

But seriously, words are as essential to our evolution as the air we breathe. As such we have had a fascination with them. From ancient times to the present day we have enjoyed playing with words and finding new ways of manipulating them; the first crossword puzzle appeared as recently as 1913. All sorts of different permutations have emerged and in this book you will find a great many of them.

But thank goodness for words, because without them we would never have had Countdown. Who would have thought that a simple parlour game would have ensconced itself into the heritage of the nation? A programme with no glitz, no big prizes, no baying audience and especially no glamorous host – how could it become an essential part of daily life for millions of people? The reason is simply our endless fascination with words. You don't have to be a clever dick to play with words. Some of our most academic contestants have failed at the first hurdle. Words belong to all of us, and each of us has our ownership rights on how we use them.

In this book there are thousands of words and hundreds of things you can do with them. In a book devoted to words and letters it's only right that the individual entries are arranged from A to Z. It's only right too that you should have a chance to put your knowledge of our language to the test and you'll find puzzles and verbal challenges cropping up in the pages that follow, with the answers (if you need them) at the back on pages 153–60.

I have to thank contestants and guests from Countdown for years of inspiration. I would like to express my thanks to the small but talented Countdown team, executive producer John Meade and producers

Michael Wylie and Mark Nyman and Clive Dickinson without whom the book would never have come about. Playing with words in this way is only fun of course, but 'fun' is a good word and I hope you have lots fun with what follows.

ABRACADABRA

No self-respecting magician would be without the magic word 'Abracadabra'. In days gone by it was used as an amulet or charm to ward off evil spirits and unpleasant diseases. People would write the word on a piece of parchment and wear it round their necks. One especially effective way of writing the charm was like this:

```
            A
          B   B
        R   R   R
      A   A   A   A
    C   C   C   C   C
  A   A   A   A   A   A
D   D   D   D   D   D   D
  A   A   A   A   A   A   A   A
B   B   B   B   B   B   B   B
  R   R   R   R   R   R   R   R   R
A   A   A   A   A   A   A   A   A   A
```

As I mentioned in the introduction we've given you a number of puzzles in the book so that you can show off your word power. In this first one your challenge is to discover how many ways is it possible to spell out the word ABRACADABRA, starting from the A at the top and always proceeding from one letter to an adjacent one? The answer is on page 153.

Of course we have our own magician on Countdown nowadays. Geoffrey Durham, besides producing moments of pure magic, demonstrates intriguing facts about numbers as well. For instance, did you know that ELEVEN PLUS TWO is an anagram of TWELVE PLUS ONE?

ABLE WAS I . . . !

'Able was I . . .' only tells you half the story – well, not quite half in fact. Complete the sentence and all is revealed:

Able was I ere I saw Elba.

Leaving aside the very unlikely possibility that Napoleon Bonaparte may have been the author of this lament, its principal interest is that the sentence reads the same backwards as it does forwards. Try it.

Real word buffs will tell you smugly that this is a popular example of a 'sotadic', named after the third-century Greek poet Sotades. Sotades is better known for the coarse verse in which he specialized. The majority of people who take an interest in these things refer to words and sentences that can be read forwards and backwards as 'palindromes', which has rather more respectable ancestry in the Greek *palin dromo*, meaning 'running back again'.

Palindrome Words

English may not boast the longest palindromic words but it has plenty of everyday ones to get you started: noon, deed, nun, kayak, civic, redder are just a few.

'Redivider' is probably the longest everyday English palindrome and 'rotavator' is well-established in horticultural circles. If you happen to be Cree Indian with a penchant for smoking a mixture of dried leaves and bark you'll be familiar with *kinnikinnik*. And in Finnish a soap-seller passes as the fifteen-letter palindrome *saippuakauppias*.

Palindrome Sentences

Had English been the first language of Eden, the first conversation might have been palindromic, and who knows what might have happened as a result.

'Madam, I'm Adam,' explained the first resident to his recently arrived companion. She, pointing at herself, replied enigmatically, 'Eve'.

The seventeenth-century Scottish author, Sir Thomas Urquart, knew something about Adam. In 1652, he published a family tree that traced the Urquarts right back to the first couple in Paradise. He gave this work the snappy title *Pantochronochanon*.

It's also claimed that Sir Thomas was something of an authority on palindromes. His universal language, details of which appeared a year after the family tree, was said to be based entirely on their use.

Sir Thomas Urquart was very much a man of his times. A staunch royalist, he is said to have died abroad 'in a fit of mirth on hearing of the Restoration' and *Chambers Biographical Dictionary* concludes, 'His learning was vast, his scholarship defective.'

Sir Thomas was in good company all the same, the first English palindromic sentence dates from his lifetime:

Lewd I did live & evil did I dwel.

With Sotades' racy pedigree the sentiment is appropriate, though the use of an ampersand and the spelling of 'dwel' take away something of its originality. A more acceptable modern version might read:

Evil I did dwell: lewd did I live.

James Thurber enjoyed creating palindromes but even his inventive genius found it a limited form of expression. 'He goddam mad dog, eh?' is his most successful.

An anonymous nineteenth-century poet came up with:

Dog as a devil deified
Deified lived as a god

Good as this is, it has to be admitted that most palindromic compositions are little more than gobbledygook. The difficulty is that once palindromes exceed fifty letters they have difficulty making sense. There are some exceptions, of course. Penelope Gilliat created the fifty-one letter palindrome:

Doc, note I dissent. A fast never prevents a fatness. I diet on cod.

Martin Gardner, the American writer on mathematics and the puzzle guru, devised another palindrome to go down the medical route:

Straw? No, too stupid a fad. I put soot on warts.

The author Leigh Mercer paid an elegant tribute to Ferdinand de

Lesseps, the builder of the Panama Canal, choosing a palindrome with which to do it:

A man, a plan, a canal: Panama!

If we followed Spanish punctuation he could have started with an exclamation mark (upside down).

These are the pick of the bunch. Others owe more to their art than their matter:

'Naomi, sex at noon taxes,' I moan.

Ten animals I slam in a net.

Some men interpret nine memos.

Sit on a potato pan, Otis.

In a regal age ran I.

Yawn a more Roman way.

Now, Ned I am a maiden won.

May a moody baby doom a yarn?

A dog! A panic in a pagoda.

Anna: 'Did Otto peep?' Otto: 'Did Anna?'

Though it would be churlish not to acknowledge that in the last of these each word in the palindrome is also a palindrome itself.

ABSENT FRIENDS

Here is a paragraph from a novel, *Gadsby*. The author, a Californian musician named Ernest Vincent Wright, dedicated it 'to Youth' with the intention that *Gadsby* would be 'a valuable aid to schoolchildren in English composition'. It only sold fifty copies so his aspirations were thwarted but *Gadsby* is remarkable for another reason, see what you make of it:

> Upon this basis I am going to show you how a bunch of bright young folks did find a champion; a man with boys and girls of his own; a man of so dominating and happy individuality that youth is drawn to him as a fly to a sugar bowl. It is not a gossipy yarn; nor is it a dry monotonous account. It is . . . a practical discarding of that worn-out notion that 'a child don't know anything'.

If you are familiar with works like this you'll realize immediately that no E is used, in fact the most commonly used vowel in English doesn't appear in any of *Gadsby's* 50,000 words. According to the author's introduction, the book was composed 'with the E type-bar of the type-writer tied down!'

If you've never come across one before – welcome to 'the lipogram', a written work composed of words chosen to avoid the use of a particular letter. We should try it on *Countdown*, it would certainly add a new dimension to the game.

Lipograms have been teasing and testing the ingenuity of writers since ancient times. As you may have guessed, the word 'lipogram' has its roots in Greek and a fifth-century Greek poet called Tryphiodorus became something of an early master of the lipogram. His greatest feat was an epic poem about the wanderings of Ulysses. This ran to twenty-four books, each named after a letter of the alphabet. The first was called *Alpha*. as you might expect. What the reader would not expect however, is that Tryphiodorus gave it that name because there wasn't a single *alpha* in the whole book. Book two was called *Beta*, because there was no *beta* and so on right through the alphabet to *Omega*. It has been suggested that the *Odyssey of Tryphiodorus* might have been improved if the poet had left out all the other letters too, but that seems a little harsh.

Down the centuries others tried their hands at the lipogram. There was Peter Riga, a canon of Notre Dame at Rheims at the end of the twelfth century. He set about writing a summary of the Old and New Testaments in twenty-three chapters. In the first chapter he avoided the letter A. The letter B was omitted from chapter two. Chapter three had to make do without C. Letter by letter the biblical summary lurched to its conclusion. As the author of the *History of Christian-Latin Poetry* commented, 'Misplaced ingenuity could go no further.'

In the sixteenth century, the Spanish poet and dramatist Lope de Vega produced five novels excluding in turn the five vowels A, E, I, O and U, finding time to do this alongside writing in excess of 1,500 plays.

Parisian theatregoers in 1816 were treated to *Pièce sans A* which promised an evening's entertainment without the assistance of the first letter of the alphabet. The story goes that the performance opened with one character announcing '*Ah, monsieur! vous voilà.*' The audience loved this and their laughter subsided just long enough for the prompter to put the actor right with, '*Eh, monsieur! vous voici*' before they were off again. History suggests that a certain amount of artistic licence was employed in this anecdote, but the fact remains that even if the play didn't open with A it certainly closed without it. The audience couldn't stay the course and the performance had to be brought to a premature conclusion.

Briefer lipograms are more acceptable. A Ross Eckler has probably achieved greater success than more ambitious lipogrammarians with his reworkings of the nursery rhyme 'Mary Had a Little Lamb'. In each case he manages to present it minus one of one of its most frequently used letters. We've seen how lipograms function without the letter E, this is Mr Eckler's 'Mary Had a Little Lamb' without an S:

> Mary had a little lamb
> With fleece a pale white hue,
> And everywhere that Mary went
> The lamb kept her in view;
> To academe he went with her,
> Illegal, and quite rare;
> It made the children laugh and play
> To view a lamb in there.

Away from Dictionary Corner on *Countdown* or the debating chamber in the House of Commons, my friend Gyles Brandreth enjoys rendering the works of Shakespeare as lipograms. Shakespeare gave Hamlet the famous soliloquy which begins:

> To be, or not to be: that is the question:
> Whether 'tis nobler in the mind to suffer
> The slings and arrows of outrageous fortune,
> Or to take arms against a sea of troubles,
> And by opposing end them? To die: to sleep;

In Gyles's version, from which I is excluded, the prince's words are changed to:

> To be, or not to be; that's the query:
> Whether you would be nobler to suffer mentally
> The stones and arrows of outrageous fortune,
> Or to take arms to oppose a sea of troubles,
> And through combat end them? To pass, to sleep;

Five acts later, with not an I in the house, Hamlet dies (sorry) fades away with the haunting line:

> The rest is hush-hush.

ALPHABETICAL ORDER

There's something very pleasing about symmetrically constructed patterns and for word enthusiasts this pattern has a special appeal.

On the left are words from one to thirteen letters long which end with all the different letters of the alphabet. On the right are another set of one- to thirteen-letter words that begin with all the different letters of the alphabet.

A	A
OB	BE
SAC	CAT
LEAD	DICE
PLATE	ELECT
SCRUFF	FIERCE
MORNING	GROCERY
HAWFINCH	HORRIBLE
SPAGHETTI	INORGANIC
DARYAOGANJ	JUXTAPOSED
STICKLEBACK	KLEPTOMANIA
TETRARCHICAL	LIQUEFACTION
PARALLELOGRAM	MICROSCOPICAL
ACCREDITATION	NEFARIOUSNESS
WHILLABALLOO	OBSTREPEROUS
THUNDERCLAP	PALINDROMIC
QARAQALPAQ	QUADRUPLET
GODMOTHER	ROUGHNECK
SLOWNESS	SYMPHONY
CONTENT	THEREIN
BUREAU	UNDONE
SCLAV	VOICE
SLOW	WILD
BOX	XED
MY	YE
Z	Z

To define the less familiar words: 'Daryoganj' is a town in India; the 'Qaraqalpaq' are a Turkic people from Central Asia; 'Sclav' is a variant spelling of 'Slav'; and 'xed' means 'marked with a cross'.

ANIMAL CRACKERS

A dog may be man's best friend but from a purely linguistic point of view man doesn't exactly return the compliment. 'Sick as a dog', 'dirty dog', 'dog-tired' , 'bitchiness' (and all the unflattering associations that go with the word) make you wonder why the canine population have put up with us for as long as they have.

Dogs aren't alone at being the butt of human abuse. How many of us would put up with being called any of these:

batty	crabby	mulish
bovine	foxy	ratty
catty	lousy	sheepish
cocky	mousy	swinish

After that dirty dozen here are a selection of other animal adjectives, less familiar for the most part and generally less offensive. Perhaps it says something about human nature that the more unpleasant animal adjectives are the ones we use most.

acciptrine	hawklike	**lutrine**	otterlike
anguine	snakelike	**murine**	mouselike
anserine	gooselike	**oscine**	songbirdlike
aquiline	eaglelike	**ovine**	sheeplike
asinine	asslike	**passerine**	perching-
caprine	goatlike		songbirdlike
cervine	deerlike	**pavonine**	peacocklike
feline	catlike	**piscine**	fishlike
herpestine	mongooselike	**porcine**	piglike
hircine	goatlike (also,	**ranine**	froglike
	especially when it	**serpentine**	serpentlike
	comes to odour and	**suilline**	hoglike
	lust)	**suine**	swinelike
lacertian	lizardlike	**taurine**	bull-like
lemurine	lemurlike	**ursine**	bearlike
leonine	lionlike	**viperine**	viperlike
lupine	wolflike	**vulpine**	foxlike

ASIA, ANTARCTICA ET AL

You've probably noticed, and if you haven't you soon will, that the names of the five continents on earth begin and end with the same letter, and in four cases out of five that letter is A: AmericA, AfricA, AntarcticA, AsiA and EuropE.

This curious coincidence set me in search of other words that also begin and end with the same letter, which resulted in this A–Z:

aloha	Jernej	says
blob	kick	tot
cynic	lull	unau
did	mum	valv
eye	nylon	wow
fluff	octavo	Xerox
gag	pip	yolky
health	Qaraqalpaq	zizz
iambi	roar	

To save you time in the dictionary; 'iambi' is the plural of 'iambus', a two-syllable line of poetry; 'Jernej' is a Serbo-Croat forename; the 'Qaraqalpaq' are the Turkic people of Central Asia we met earlier; 'unau' is a species of South American sloth; 'valv' is a reformed spelling of 'valve'.

AUTHOR, AUTHOR

On Countdown we're no strangers to writers and their works but we don't (yet) ask competitors to come up with authors who have names that are particularly appropriate for certain books. But here are twenty top titles that would catch anyone's eye as they browse along a bookshelf:

The American South by Louise Yanner
The Antiques by Fay Kingham
The Barmaid by Phyllis Glass
Better Gardening by Anita Lawn
Carpet Fitting by Walter Wall
Central Heating by Bernie Coles and Ray D Aytor
The Cliff Tragedy by Eileen Dover
Consumer Guide to Credit by Owen Munny
Cutting It Fine by Moses Lawn
Dental Surgery by Phil McAvity
Diagonals by Criss Cross
Household Repairs by Andy Mann
The Housing Problem by Rufus Quick
A Life of Crime by Robin Banks
On the Rebound by Rick O'Shea
Painting and Decorating by Matt Coats
Rural Transport by Orson Cart
Slimming by Lena Bodie
Springtime by Teresa Green
The Woman Who Sang by Topsy Sharp

Although one wouldn't find any of these authors on Countdown, we do have our fair share of scribes: Nigel Rees, Sheridan Morley, Richard Stilgoe (children's books), Simon Williams, Michael Parkinson and last, but by no means least, Yorkshire's own world best-seller – Barbara Taylor Bradford. And Simon Mason, one of England's leading young authors, did a spell in Dictionary Corner.

BLOOMER, BOWDLER AND BOYCOTT

In the last fifty years English has been enriched, if that's the word, with: beatlemania, quisling, Thatcherite and Stalinist – four examples of a substantial vocabulary of eponyms, or words that owe their origin to the names or nicknames of real people.

The exuberant adoration that greeted the Fab Four gave us 'beatlemania'; Norway's wartime fascist leader, Vidkun Quisling, gave us a new noun for a treacherous collaborator; Britain's first woman prime minister gave us an adjective to epitomize her political philosophy; and the wartime premier of the USSR adopted a name meaning 'man of steel' in Russian, which provided posterity with a word that will always recall his political doctrine and practice.

The origins of similar words are not as easily identified, in fact some words have become so absorbed into the language that the links with their originators have been virtually forgotten. To cast a little light on some of them, here are a couple of dozen familiar words with biographical sketches of the people who made them famous:

amp   André Ampère (1775–1836), French mathematician and physicist who undertook pioneering work in electricity. The electrical unit ampere (amp) was named after him.

bloomer   Amelia Jenks Bloomer (1818–94), American feminist writer and reformer, who popularized as a fashion statement the form of trousers for women which bear her name.

bowdlerize   Thomas Bowdler (1754–1825), London doctor who took it upon himself prudishly to edit the works of Shakespeare, a ten-volume undertaking from which 'those words and expressions are omitted which cannot with propriety be read aloud in a family'. Dr Bowdler did the same with *Gibbon's Decline and Fall of the Roman Empire*.

bowie knife   James Bowie (1790–1836), American pioneer who invented the curved sheath-knife named after him. He was killed at the battle of the Alamo.

boycott   Charles Boycott (1832–97), English land agent in Ireland who was one of the first to be socially excommunicated by Irish followers of Charles Stewart Parnell.

braille   Louis Braille (1809–52), blind from the age of three, became a professor at a school for the blind in Paris and developed the system of raised-point writing named after him.

bunsen burner   Robert Wilhelm Bunsen (1811–99), German chemist who invented several scientific instruments, most famous of which was the gas burner that bears his name.

chauvinist   Nicholas Chauvin, a French soldier in Napoleon's army. He was wounded seventeen times only to be retired on a paltry pension. In spite of this, his devotion to the emperor remained undimmed and he worshipped him uncritically.

derrick   Thomas Derrick (c 1600) was a hangman whose professional relationship with the gallows led to his association with the long-pivoted beam used for hoisting heavy objects.

diesel   Rudolf Diesel (1858–1913), German engineer at the Krupps factory, who in 1897 invented the first practical compression-ignition engine, which ran on cheap crude oil. The diesel engine is named after him.

dunce   John Duns Scotus (c 1265–1308), Scottish philosopher and one of the most significant theologians of the Middle Ages. He was anything but a dunce in the modern sense, but adversaries referred to his followers disparagingly as 'Dunses' for their hair-splitting pedantry.

galvanize   Luigi Galvani (1737–98), Italian physiologist who made frogs' legs twitch by 'galvanizing' them through connecting leg muscles to their corresponding nerves. The modern meaning 'to stimulate strongly' reflects this original experiment.

guillotine   Joseph Guillotin (I738–1814), French doctor who advocated a more humane form of capital punishment. The 'guillotine' named after him was designed and built by others.

leotard   Jules Léotard (I830–70), French trapeze artist who had this tight-fitting, one-piece garment worn for dancing and exercise named after him.

macadam   John McAdam (1756–1836), Scottish engineer who developed a system of road construction using crushed stone, bound with gravel and raised, to improve drainage.

martinet   Jean Martinet (d 1672), French military engineer and commander, 'accidentally' killed in action by his troops who resented his brutal sense of discipline.

maverick   Samuel Maverick (1803–70), early Texan settler of independent disposition. His cattle ventures ended with large numbers of unbranded livestock wandering the range freely. Neighbours called all the unbranded cattle 'mavericks' and the name stuck with Texas cowboys.

mesmerize   Friedrich Anton Mesmer (I734–1815), Austrian doctor who founded the hypnotic treatment known as 'mesmerism'.

pasteurize   Louis Pasteur (1822–95), French chemist and father of modern bacteriology who, among many other things, developed the process of pasteurization which heats milk long enough to kill germs but not enough to ruin the taste.

pullman car   George Mortimer Pullman (1831–97), American inventor and businessman who designed the Pullman railroad sleeping-car, patented 1864–5.

sandwich   John Montagu, 4th Earl of Sandwich (1718–92). The Sandwich Islands were named after him by Captain Cook. Lord Sandwich was First Lord of the Admiralty from 1748–51. He was an inveterate gambler and used to chew on a slice of meat between two pieces of bread as he sat at the gaming table – hence the 'sandwich'.

saxophone   Antoine Joseph Saxe (1814–94), Belgian musician and inventor, who invented several brass wind instruments, the most successful of which was the saxophone, patented in 1845.

shrapnel   Henry Shrapnel (1761–1842), English artillery officer and inventor of the exploding shell.

sideburns   Ambrose Everett Burnside (I824 –8I), American Civil War commander who lent his name to a style of side-whiskers first called 'burnsides' and later 'sideburns'.

teddy bear   Theodore Roosevelt (1858–1919), hunting once in, Mississippi the US president spared the life of a bear cub. From this act of kindness sprang the affection for the teddy bear.

BOAT BENEATH A
SUNNY SKY

An acrostic is a verse in which a word, message, or most commonly, a name, is spelled out by the initial letters of each line.

Lewis Carroll was mad about acrostics and his most famous one was written for Alice Pleasance Liddell, the Alice who inspired *Alice's Adventures in Wonderland*:

A boat, beneath a sunny sky
Lingering onward dreamily
In an evening of July –

Children three that nestle near,
Eager eye and willing ear,
Pleased a simple tale to hear –

Long has paled the sunny sky;
Echoes fade and memories die:
Autumn frosts have slain July.

Still she haunts me, phantomwise,
Alice moving under skies
Never seen by waking eye.

Children yet the tale to hear,
Eager eye and willing ear,
Lovingly shall nestle near.

In Wonderland they lie,
Dreaming as the days go by,
Dreaming as the summers die:

Ever drifting down the stream –
Lingering in the golden gleam –
Life, what is it but a dream?

Acrostics were popular with Victorians as puzzles as well as verses. Queen Victoria herself was very taken with double acrostics and she is credited with the authorship of this geographic puzzle 'for the royal children', which presumably did amuse her.

The initial letters spell out the name of a town in Great Britain and the last letters spell, in reverse order, something for which it is famous. Can you work out where it is? (Answer on page 153.)

A city in Italy

A river in Germany

A town in the United States

A town in North America

A town in Holland

The Turkish name of Constantinople

A town in Bothnia

A city in Greece

A circle on the globe

BOXING CLEVER

Sam Lloyd was one of the great masters of puzzledom and the box puzzles he devised are among his most popular.

This alphabet-box puzzle is a test of both logic and patience. Cut out nine squares of card or paper, mark them with the letters A, B, C, D, E, F, G and H and arrange them in a box like this:

G	E	F
H	C	B
D		A

The challenge now is to return them to their correct alphabetical order, moving one square at a time (you'll find the shortest solution on page 153):

you'll find the shortest solution on page 153

```
A   B   C
D   E   F
G   H
```

BRUNCH AT THE MOTEL

People had been enjoying breakfast at around lunchtime long before 1896 when the word 'brunch' was usefully coined to describe this particular meal. They'd also been stopping off at roadside accommodation catering for drivers and their passengers before 1925 when 'motel' entered the language.

Both 'brunch' and 'motel' are examples of what Lewis Carroll termed a 'portmanteau', a word created by packing together two other words. One of his own most successful portmanteaus came from melding 'gallop' and 'triumph' to form the suitably Carrollian word 'galumph'.

Now for a selection of portmanteaus that have entered the language since Carroll's day:

anecdotard	anecdote + dotard, a dotard prone to telling anecdotes
beautility	beauty + utility
botel	boat + hotel
cheeseburger	cheese + hamburger
citrange	citrus + orange
diplonomics	diplomacy + economics, use of economic power for diplomatic ends
gasid indigestion	gas + indigestion, a minor medical condition
glommentary	glossary + commentary
liger	lion + tiger, the offspring of a lion and a tigress
macon	mutton + bacon, mutton salted and smoked like bacon, and consumed during the Second World War
mocamp	motor + camp, establishment with parking and camping facilities
stagflation	stagnation + inflation, zero economic growth with rising inflation

C PLUS

This is a puzzle to test word power and anagram skills, the hallmarks of all who grace *Countdown!* Though I imagine this wouldn't be much of a challenge to *Countdown* co-producer, Mark Nyman who, in 1993 became the World Scrabble Champion. Indeed, most of the Scrabble elite have appeared on *Countdown*.

If you add C to each of these words and rearrange the letters you can form a new word. By adding another C and again rearranging the letters you can make a third word. As an example, if you add C to ESAU it's possible to create CAUSE. When another C is added and the letters are shuffled, up comes ACCUSE.

The trick is to try to form words that are neither plurals or verbs ending with S. See how you get on with these (answers on pages 153–4):

ark	irk	nose	rose
hat	lean	oast	sear
hate	lout	oil	sour
head	near	oust	spite
here	neat	rile	tape

COUNTDOWN = QUIZ

'Countdown', the equals sign =, and 'quiz' belong to a group of invented words that have interesting stories to tell.

In the case of 'countdown' it was the arrival of science-fiction films that popularized the word for backward counting leading to the start of an event. According to one source 'countdown' was first used in a film directed by the pioneer science-fiction film-maker Fritz Lang.

The equals sign has a longer pedigree. The sixteenth-century mathematician Robert Recorde was scratching round for a suitable symbol for equality when he hit on the idea of using a pair of parallel lines. 'No 2 thynges,' he explained, 'can be more equal than 2 parallel straight lines' and his algebra work *The Whetstone of Witte* was the first publication to use the equals sign =.

'Quiz' appropriately poses a question about its origins. Although lexicographers can point to conflicting evidence, the popular anecdote sets the birth of the new word in eighteenth-century Dublin. There the theatre manager James Daly took on a bet that he could invent and instantly popularize a new meaningless word. His next step was to hire a gang of Dublin street children to chalk 'quiz' on walls throughout the city. In no time at all every Dubliner had seen the mysterious word and since no one had a clue what it meant 'quiz' became associated with a mental test and it hasn't looked back.

COINING IT IN

We have had several words on *Countdown* which contestants have tried and which have sounded as though they should be in the dictionary.

'Steaked' was suggested by Tim Morrisey, the Dublin Wonderkid. Definition: what happens to a cow when it is made into steaks.

'Moggied' was Gweni Sorokin's inspired offering. Definition: what has happened to you when the cats have taken over your house and/or, your life.

'Tiggles' was another 'cat' word tried by Martin Coxell. Possible definition: cat giggles.

'Snailed' was a word Kathryn Barratt came up with. Possible definition: a description of how a line of school children approached their least favourite lesson.

Other words that have been offered and sounded as though they should be allowed are:

beloving	homaged	stonked
blarier	impaler	tinkler
desirer	inversed	tivot
dopish	moilers	tonely
dullens	plaiders	wagger
gainly	refelt	winless
grovers	spraint	
hearted	squidge	

If any of these words do find their way into the language to be officially recognized in dictionaries, *Countdown* and the contestants will be in good company. William Shakespeare was the first to use over 1,700 words, among them: auspicious, assassination, bump, critic, road and livery.

Other well-known word inventors include:

Jeremy Bentham, who gave us: international, maximize and minimize.

Robert Boyle, who gave us: intensity and pendulum.

29

Edmund Burke, who gave us: diplomacy, electioneering, federalism and municipality.

Thomas Carlyle, who gave us: self-help.

Lewis Carroll, who gave us: brunch, chortle, flimsy and squawk.

Winston Churchill, who gave us: United Nations. which he found in a poem by Byron.

Samuel Taylor Coleridge, who gave us: intensify.

COUNTING ON ME

On Countdown we like to think we stretch our contestants mathematically as well as verbally. So I was pleased to discover, thanks to the numerate verbivore Darryl Francis, that quite a few numbers successfully double as words. For example, 'forty-nine' is a customer in an American diner who leaves without paying, 'sixty-six' is a two-handed card game and 'seventy-four' is a type of South African fish. To give a flavour of what the world of numbers can do for your vocabulary here are twenty-five examples to get you started:

zero	a place in Lauderdale County, Mississippi
one	the ultimate being
two	a two-dollar bill
three	a rugby three-quarter
four	a type of racing boat
five	a basketball team
six	a high-scoring shot in cricket
seven	the rower sitting behind the stroke in an –
eight	the racing boat in which they row
nine	a baseball team
ten	a measure of coal, from 48 to 50 tons
eleven	a football or cricket team
twelve	a shilling
thirteen	an Irish term for an English shilling
fourteen	a special order
fifteen	a Rugby Union team
sixteen	a place in Meagher County, Montana
seventeen	a corpse
eighteen	the size of a piece of paper cut eighteen from a sheet
nineteen	the score of zero in cribbage
twenty	a twenty-dollar bill
twenty-one	limeade
twenty-two	rifle or pistol with a .22 calibre
twenty-three	the end
twenty-four	a day
twenty-five	a variety of spoil-five

CRYPTARITHMETIC

When is a letter of the alphabet not a letter? The answer is when it's a number.

In these puzzles each letter represents a different digit. See if you can work out which letter represents which digit(answers on page 154).

1
```
   E
   E
  E+
 ──
  ME
```

2
```
   O
  NO +
 ──
  ON
```

3
```
 SEND
 MORE+
 ─────
 MONEY
```

4
```
   TEN
   TEN
 FORTY+
 ──────
 SIXTY
```

5
```
   TWO
 THREE
 SEVEN +
 ──────
 TWELVE
```

DIARY DIRGE

From January to December, this anonymous author composed a dozen thought-provoking verses with the arresting title 'Janet was quite ill one day':

> JANet was quite ill one day.
>
> FEBrile troubles came her way.
>
> MARtyr-like, she lay in bed;
>
> APRoned nurses softly sped.
>
> MAYbe, said the leech judicial,
>
> JUNket would be beneficial.
>
> JULeps, too, though freely tried,
>
> AUGured ill, for Janet died.
>
> SEPulchre was sadly made;
>
> OCTaves pealed and prayers were said.
>
> NOVices with many a tear
>
> DECorated Janet's bier.

DICTIONARY WITH A DIFFERENCE

No work on words would be complete, or satisfying, if it didn't include an acknowledgement to Ambrose Bierce, one of America's most original men of letters. Today Bierce is largely remembered for the *Devil's Dictionary*, which he published a century ago. As a journalist and humorous writer, he worked for weeklies in California before joining the staff of the English magazine *Fun* at the beginning of 1872. Four years later he was back in San Francisco writing for the *Sunday Examiner* where he grew to become, in the words on one biographical note, 'a sort of literary dictator of the Pacific Coast'.

The *Devil's Dictionary* dates from this time and reflects Bierce's astringent attitude to life. Sardonic and acerbic he may appear but his dictionary offers a wickedly trenchant view of the human condition.

The man who defined 'a cynic' as 'a blackguard whose faulty vision sees things as they are, not as they ought to be' disappeared in Mexico in 1913. He was seventy-one and announced before his departure that he was leaving 'with a pretty definite purpose, which, however, is not at present disclosable'. Bierce was never heard from again but the *Devil's Dictionary* remains as an enduring memorial to him. Here are some of its many entertaining and arresting entries:

acquaintance   a person whom we know well enough to borrow from, but not well enough to lend to.

alliance   in international politics, the union of two thieves who have their hands so deeply inserted in each other's pockets that they cannot separately plunder a third.

bigot   one who is obstinately and zealously attached to an opinion that you do not entertain.

bore   a person who talks when you wish him to listen.

clergyman   a man who undertakes the management of our spiritual affairs as a method of bettering his temporal ones.

connoisseur a specialist who knows everything about something and nothing about anything else.

duty that which sternly impels us in the direction of profit, along the line of desire.

economy purchasing the barrel of whisky that you do not need for the price of the cow that you cannot afford.

excess in morale, an indulgence that enforces by appropriate penalties the law of moderation.

fidelity a virtue peculiar to those who are about to be betrayed.

grammar a system of pitfalls thoughtfully prepared for the feet of the self-made man, along the path by which he advances to distinction.

heaven a place where the wicked cease from troubling you with talk of their personal affairs, and the good listen with attention while you expound your own.

ignoramus a person unacquainted with certain kinds of knowledge familiar to yourself, and having certain other kinds that you know nothing about.

jury unduly concerned about the preservation of that which can be lost only if worth keeping.

logic the art of thinking and reasoning in strict accordance with the limitations and incapacities of the human misunderstanding.

misfortune the kind of fortune that never misses.

opposition in politics the party that prevents the government from running amuck by hamstringing it.

optimist a proponent of the doctrine that black is white.

quantity a good substitute for quality when you are hungry.

selfish devoid of consideration for the selfishness of others.

success	the one unpardonable sin against one's fellows.
take	to acquire, frequently by force but preferably by stealth.
truth	an ingenious compound of desirability and appearance.
ultimatum	in diplomacy, a last demand before resorting to concessions.
yesterday	the infancy of youth, the youth of manhood, the entire past of age.
zeal	a certain nervous disorder afflicting the young and inexperienced.

Countdown regular, Philip Franks (actor, theatre director, lover of word games), through giving a definition from the *Devil's Dictionary* on each of his appearances, aroused so much interest in the *Devil's Dictionary* that the publishers decided to reprint it. Philip also likes to play a variety of word games as we go into the break. Have a go at this one (answers on page 155):

Name ten films with different American states in their titles.

DISPROPORTIONABLE INCOMPREHENSIBILITIES

This may be a bit of a mouthful but these two words represent two of the longest English words in regular use – 'disproportionableness' and 'incomprehensibilities'.

Both are twenty-one letters long. From there on, word length is in inverse proportion to frequency of word use. Here are some examples:

interdenominationalism (22 letters)

honorificabilitudinitatibus (27 letters) The word means 'with honour-ablenesses' and appears in Shakespeare's play *Love's Labour's Lost*.

antidisestablishmentarianism (28 letters) Gladstone is reported to have included this in his vocabulary. It means a 'doctrine of opposition to disestablishment (withdrawal of state patronage, support, or exclusive recognition from a church).

floccipaucinihilipilification (29 letters) The longest word listed in the *Oxford English Dictionary* means 'the action of estimating as worthless'. First recorded in 1741, Sir Walter Scott later found a use for it.

praetertranssubstantiationalistically (37 letters) This was used in the novel *Untimely Ripped* by Mark McShane, published in 1963. It means the act of surpassing the act of transubstantiation, referring specifically to the transformation of bread and wine into the blood and body of Christ during mass in the Roman Catholic faith.

hepaticocholangiocholecystenterostimies (39 letters) If you have had surgery to create new communications between your gall bladder and hepatic duct and between your intestines and your gall bladder, this is the medical term for what you've had done.

pneumonoultramicroscopicsilicovolcanoconiosis (45 letters) This is a condition found among miners in particular. It is a lung disease caused by the inhalation of very fine silica dust.

DOUBLE OR QUINQUENNIUM

A 'quinquennium' is both a period of five years and also one of the few words in which the letter Q is used twice.

There are many words in which a particular letter appears twice, so far this sentence has five (six if you count 'sentence'). From A–Z, here are twenty-six words that use at least one letter twice:

a	baa	**n**	inn
b	ebb	**o**	coo
c	cock	**p**	pip
d	did	**q**	quinquennium
e	see	**r**	err
f	off	**s**	ass
g	gag	**t**	tot
h	high	**u**	usual
i	icicle	**v**	valve
j	jejune	**w**	wow
k	kick	**x**	executrix
l	all	**y**	yolky
m	mum	**z**	jazz

Increase the frequency to three and the task becomes significantly more difficult, but it can be done:

a	banana	**n**	nanny
b	bobby	**o**	ovolo
c	coccyx	**p**	poppy
d	daddy	**q**	Qaraqalpaq
e	epee	**r**	error
f	fluff	**s**	sass
g	giggle	**t**	tatty
h	heighth	**u**	unusual
i	iiwi	**v**	viva-voce
j	Jijjin	**w**	powwow
k	kakariki	**x**	hexahydroxycyclohexane
l	lull	**y**	syzygy
m	mummy	**z**	zizz

'Heighth', in case you didn't know, is a dialectal spelling of 'height'; an 'iiwi' is a brightly coloured bird found in Hawaii; 'Jijjin' is a town in Jordan; a 'kakariki' is a type of parakeet and also a New Zealand lizard; 'hexahydroxycyclohexane' is worth getting to know – it's a chemical component of the vitamin B complex and, as such, essential for life; and 'zizz', in case you didn't know, is a whirring sound.

DOUBLE RIDDLES

Two riddles are shown here and each has two equally valid answers (on page 155). Your challenge is to find both.

1 My first is in *split* but not in *tear*;
  My second's in *apple* and also in *pear*;
  My third is in *bitter* but is not in *sour*;
  My fourth is in *moment* but is not in *hour*;
  My fifth is in *quadrant* as well as in *square*;
  My sixth is in *circus* but is not in *fair*;
  My seventh's in *shine* and also in *sheen*;
  My whole, you will see, has leaves that are green.

2 My first is in *rabbit* but is not in *hare*;
  My second's in *brace* but is not in *pair*;
  My third is in *ladder* but is not in *climb*;
  My fourth is in *lemon* and also in *lime*;
  My fifth is in *aunt* but is not in *niece*
  My sixth is in *gander* but is not in *geese*;
  My seventh is seen both in *grandma* and *daughter*;
  My whole is an island surrounded by water.

EMPLOYMENT SOUGHT

In 1842 income tax made an unwelcome return to these islands, the *Illustrated London News* was first published and this unusual advertisement appeared in *The Times*:

TO WIDOWERS AND SINGLE GENTLEMEN – WANTED by a lady, a SITUATION to superintend the household and preside at table. She is Agreeable, Becoming, Careful, Desirable, English, Facetious [which in those days meant witty and amusing], Generous, Honest, Industrious, [J was considered an optional letter at that time], Keen, Lively, Merry, Natty, Obedient, Philosophic, Quiet, Regular, Sociable, Tasteful, Useful, Vivacious, Womanish, Xantippish, Youthful, Zealous, &c.

If these weren't qualifications enough, the lady surely commended herself as an accomplished alphabetician, one who succeeded in writing a sentence in which each word began with a successive letter of the alphabet.

ENIGMA VARIATIONS

'Enigma' was the name given to the encryption machine used by German cryptographers during the Second World War. British intelligence used an early form of computer code named Colossus to decode Enigma encryptions. Colossus was able to sift through the thousands of code permutations that Enigma had generated apparently at random. By this means it was able to crack German coded messages far faster than human codebreakers.

In more primitive coding systems understanding a few principles about the relative frequencies in a language can be an invaluable tool to deciphering a secret message. Applying these ten rules would help crack a code written in English.

1   Letters of highest frequency in descending order are: E, T, A, O, N, I, R, S, H. (These account for about seventy per cent of any English text.)

2   Letters of medium frequency in descending order are: D, L, U, C, M.

3   Letters of low frequency in descending order are: P, F, Y, W, G, B, V.

4   Letters of lowest frequency, in descending order: K, X, Q, J, Z.

5   Vowels will account for about forty per cent of the letters in a given text.

6   Half of the words in English begin with: A, O, S, T, W.

7   Half of all the words in English end with: D, E, S, T.

8   In English the most frequently used double letters are: EE, FF, OO, SS, TT.

9   Other common doubles are: CC, MM, NN, PP, RR.

10 Using a basis of 10,000 word-counts, the ten commonest words in English, arranged by letter totals, are in order of frequency:
    Two-letter: of, to, in, it, is, be, as, at, so, we.
    Three-letter: the, and, for, are, but, not, you, all, any, can.
    Four-letter: that, with, have, this, will, your, from, they, know, want.

EON, TOW, THERE . . .

With numbers playing their part on *Countdown* it seemed only right to investigate how they cross over with words when you form anagrams with number names.

Take 'one hundred' for instance, which you can turn into 'under-honed', not a word you'll find in a dictionary, I admit, but one with an obvious meaning to anyone who has ever tried cutting anything with an inadequately sharpened tool.

Not all the anagrams are as easy to find as those for 'one', 'two' and 'three', from four to twenty some are obscure and a few come from foreign languages, but an anagram is an anagram when all's said and done.

one	eon
two	tow
three	there
four	rouf (obsolete form of 'roof' and 'rough')
five	veif (Old Norse for something flapping or waving)
six	xis (plural of xi, the fourteenth letter of the Greek alphabet)
seven	evens
eight	teigh (obsolete form of the past tense of 'tee', meaning to draw)
nine	nein ('nine' in the fourteenth century and the German for 'no')
ten	net
eleven	Levene (surname, among others that of pioneering American biochemist Aaron Theodore Levene, whose work included some preliminary work on the identification of DNA)
twelve	velwet (form of spelling 'velvet' in the fifteenth and sixteenth centuries)
thirteen	threiten (Scots form of 'threaten')

fourteen	neetrouf (slang form of 'fourteen')
fifteen	fiftene (medieval spelling of 'fifteen')
sixteen	sextine (a type of poem)
seventeen	seventene (Middle English form of 'seventeen')
eighteen	teheeing (present participle of 'teehee' meaning to titter)
nineteen	ninetene (fourteenth-century spelling of 'nineteen')
twenty	twynte (spelling of 'twynt', an obsolete noun meaning a jot or particle)

FIGURE IT OUT

Did you know that calculators can spell? I'm not talking about the sort of impressive personal organizer which sort out your life, give you the word you're looking for in five different languages and perform any known mathematical calculation. No, the calculator I have in mind is the simple one you use for working out sums you can't manage on the back of an envelope. Calculators like this aren't designed to spell of course, but with a little lateral thinking they can create a surprisingly wide vocabulary.

The trick lies in reading certain numbers upside down so that they read like letters. Nine letters can be obtained by using nine numbers like this:

To get **B** enter **8**

To get **E** enter **3**

To get **G** enter **6** (for a capital G enter 9)

To get **H** enter **4**

To get **I** enter **I**

To get **L** enter **7**

To get **O** enter **0**

To get **S** enter **5**

To get **Z** enter **2**

Since the words on the calculator have to be read upside down, the numbers/letters must be entered in reverse order.

Once you've mastered these words, you'll have fun discovering others by applying the same rules:

To spell **BEE** enter **338**

To spell **BEG** enter **938**

To spell **BLESS** enter **55378**

To spell **BOBBLE** enter **378808**

To spell **BOGGLE** enter **379908**

To spell **BOIL** enter **7108**

To spell **EGG** enter **993**

To spell **GEESE** enter **35339**

To spell **GIGGLE** enter **379919**

To spell **GLEE** enter **3379**

To spell **GOBBLE** enter **378809**

To spell **GOSH** enter **4509**

To spell **HE** enter **34**

To spell **HILL** enter **7714**

To spell **HISS** enter **5514**

To spell **HOSE** enter **3504**

To spell **ILL** enter **771**

To spell **LESS** enter **5537**

To spell **LOG** enter **907**

To spell **LOOSE** enter **35007**

To spell **LOSE** enter **3507**

To spell **LOSS** enter **5507**

To spell **OBOE** enter **3080**

To spell **SEIZE** enter **32135**

To spell **SELL** enter **7735**

To spell **SHELL** enter **77345**

To spell **SHOE** enter **3045**

To spell **SIEGE** enter **39315**

To spell **SIGH** enter **4615**

To spell **SIZE** enter **3215**

To spell **SLOSH** enter **45075**

To spell **SOB** enter **805**

FLIT ON CHEERING ANGEL!

'Flit on cheering angel!' was the anagram Lewis Carroll thought up for Florence Nightingale. In this respect Richard Stilgoe is a present-day Lewis Carroll, a master at rearranging people's names in a wonderfully creative way.

There are several anagrams of Richard Whiteley:

> dirty wheelchair
> wild charity here
> a wiry child there
> ideal with cherry
> hail, dry wit, cheer!

My favourite is . . .

> lecher with diary

Here are some other prime targets for the anagrammist:

Roald Amundsen	laud'd Norseman
Madame Curie	radium came
Clint Eastwood	Old West action
Dwight D Eisenhower	Wow! he's right indeed!
Indira Gandhi	had Indian rig
Henry Wadsworth Longfellow	won half the new world's glory
Ronald Reagan	an oral danger
Dante Gabriel Rosetti	greatest idealist born
William Shakespeare	I ask me, has Will a peer?
Margaret Thatcher	great charm threat
Mary Whitehouse	I may rue the show

FRIGHT OF YOUR LIFE

'Agoraphobia' the fear of open spaces, 'claustrophobia' the fear of enclosed spaces and 'hydrophobia' the fear of water are conditions that a good many people would recognize. But there are other common anxieties like 'dromophobia' the fear of crossing streets, 'photophobia' the fear of strong light and 'sideredromophobia', the fear of travelling by train which have names that most of us have never heard of.

Looking down a list of medical conditions there seem to be phobias for just about anything from the number thirteen, 'terdekaphobia' to dawn, 'eosophobia', and from pleasure, 'hedonophobia', to ideas, 'ideophobia'. There's even 'logophobia', the fear of words, but we don't have much to do with that on *Countdown*.

To give an idea of the sort of phobias around, fifty are listed with their causes:

animals	zoophobia	**fur**	doraphobia
auroral lights	auroraphobia	**glass bottoms**	hyalinopygophobia
beards	pogonophobia	**going to bed**	clinophobia
blushing	erythrophobia	**heredity**	patroiophobia
cheerfulness	cherophobia	**home**	oikophobia
clouds	nephophobia	**human beings**	anthropophobia
crowds	ochlophobia	**imperfection**	atelophobia
dampness	hygrophobia	**infinity**	apeirophobia
dreams	oneirophobia	**justice**	dikephobia
drink	potophobia	**leaves**	phyllophobia
everything	panphobia	**marriage**	gamophobia
eyes	ommatophobia	**narrowness**	anginophobia
fall of man made satellites	keraunothnetophobia	**nudity**	gymnophobia
		one thing	monophobia
feathers	pteronophobia	**points**	aichurophobia
flashes	selaphobia	**poverty**	peniaphobia
flute	aulophobia	**responsibility**	hypegiaphobia

49

ridicule	katagelophobia	**void**	kenophobia
shadows	sciophobia	**walking**	bathophobia
sitting idle	thaasophobia	**weakness**	asthenophobia
speaking aloud	phonophobia	**wind**	ancraophobia
string	linonophobia	**women**	gynophobia
taste	geumatophobia	**work**	ergophobia
teeth	odontophobia	**writing**	graphophobia
thinking	phronemophobia	**young girls**	parthenophobia
vehicles	ochophobia		

FROM HEAD TO TAIL

If Lewis Carroll were alive today he'd be a great asset in Dictionary Corner and having a university maths lecturer on Countdown would let me off the hook when the numbers come round!

From an early age Lewis Carroll was fascinated by word games. He invented lots of them and Doublets, the game in which you have to transform one word into another in a given number of steps, is one of his most popular.

Doublets first appeared in 1879 when Carroll wrote to the editor of Vanity Fair:

Dear Vanity, – Just a year ago last Christmas, two young ladies – smarting under that sorest scourge of feminine humanity, the having 'nothing to do' – besought me to send them 'some riddles'. But riddles I had none at hand, and therefore set myself to devise some other form of verbal torture which should serve the same purpose. The result of my meditations was a new kind of Puzzle – new at least to me – which, now that it has been fairly tested by a year's experience, and commended by many friends, I offer to you, as a newly-gathered nut, to be cracked by the omnivorous teeth which have already masticated so many of your Double Acrostics.

The rules of the Puzzle are simple enough. Two words are proposed, of the same length; and the Puzzle consists in linking these together by interposing other words, each of which shall differ from the next word *in one letter only.* That is to say, one letter may be changed in one of the given words, then one letter in the word so obtained, and so on, till we arrive at the other given word. The letters must not be interchanged among themselves, but each must keep to its own place. As an example, the word 'head' may be changed into 'tail' by interposing the words 'heal, teal, tell, tall'. I call the two given words 'a Doublet', the interposed words 'Links', and the entire series 'a Chain', of which I here append an example:

HEAD
heal
teal
tell
tall
TAIL

It is, perhaps, needless to state that it is *de rigeur* that the links should be English words, such as might be used in good society.

The easiest Doublets are those in which the consonants in one word answer to consonants in the other, and the vowels to vowels; 'head' and 'tail' constitute a Doublet of this kind. Where this is not the case, as in 'head' and 'hare', the first thing to be done is to transform one member of the Doublet into a word whose consonants and vowels shall answer to those in the other member (e.g.' head, herd, here,') after which there is seldom much difficulty in completing the Chain.

I am told that there is an American game involving a similar principle. I have never seen it, and can only say of its inventors, *pereant qui ante nos nostra dixerunt!*   Lewis Carroll

Puzzles in *Vanity Fair* had been going through a dull patch and the arrival of Doublets brought new life to the puzzle section. Three trial Doublets were run before the first competition Doublet was set on 19 April 1879. The response was enthusiastic, though sometimes acrimonious as several thousand competitors took issue with Carroll's choice of words. His response was to publish a glossary of 1,400 words of from three to six letters. He prefaced this with a piece he had already written to *Vanity Fair* about the sort of words he regarded as ineligible:

Choker humbly presents his compliments to the four thousand three hundred and seventeen (or thereabouts) indignant Doubleteers who have so strongly shent him, and pre to being soaked in the spate of their wrath, asks for a fiver of minutes for reflection. Choker is in a state of complete pye. He feels that there must be a stent to the admission of spick words. He is quite unable to sweal the chaffy spelt, to stile the pory cole, or to swill a spate from a piny ait to the song of the spink. Frills and the mystic Gole are strangers in his sheal: the chanceful Gord hath never brought him gold, nor ever did a cate become his ain. The Doubleteers will no doubt spank him sore, with slick quotations and wild words of yore, will pour upon his head whole steres of steens and poods of spiles points downwards/ But he trusts that those alone who habitually use such words as these in good society, and whose discourse is universally there understood, will be the first to cast a stean at him.

Carroll set three Doublets a week in *Vanity Fair*. These are the first two dozen. The answers are on pages 155–7 but, before turning to them, see how you match up against Victorian puzzlers from the spring of 1879:

1   Drive PIG into STY with four links

2   Raise FOUR to FIVE with six links

3   Make WHEAT into BREAD with six links

4   Dip PEN into INK with five links

5   Touch CHIN with NOSE with five links

6   Change TEARS into SMILE with five links

7   Change WET into DRY with three links

8   Make HARE into SOUP with six links

9   PITCH TENTS with five links

10   Cover EYE with LID with three links

11   Prove PITY to be GOOD with six links

12   STEAL COINS with seven links

13   Make EEL into PIE with three links

14   Turn POOR into RICH with five links

15   Prove RAVEN to be MISER with three links

16   Change OAT to RYE with three links

17   Get WOOD from TREE with seven links

18   Prove GRASS to be GREEN with seven links

19   Evolve MAN from APE with five links

20   Change CAIN into ABEL with eight links

21   Make FLOUR into BREAD with five links

22   Make TEA HOT with three links

23   Run COMB into HAIR with six links

24   Prove ROGUE to be a BEAST with ten links

FULL HOUSE

I wonder what contestants think when they see Carol turning up their letters on *Countdown*. For instance which vowel are they really hoping for when they ask for one?

Creating words that use all five vowels A, E, I, O, and U might be good practice. In 'abstemious' the five vowels appear in alphabetical order. Here are twenty other examples, where the vowels are used in a different order. How many others are there, I wonder?

aeiou	facetious
aioue	anxiousness
auioe	auctioned, cautioned
eouai	encouraging
euaio	equation, refutation, reputation, education
euoia	euphoria, pneumonia, sequoia
iaoue	dialogue
iouae	discourage, inoculate
oauie	consanguine
oeaui	overhauling
oueai	housemaid
uaioe	ultraviolet
uoiae	unsociable

GOODBYE TO ALL THAT

Robert Graves, poet, professor, author of *I, Claudius* and *Claudius the God*, as well as his autobiography *Goodbye to All That*, had a fondness for traditional means of expression whether it be metres, rhymes or words, as these verses prove:

> Gone are the drab monosyllabic days
> When 'agricultural labour' still was *tilth*;
> And '100 per cent approbation' *praise*;
> And 'pornographic modernism', *filth* –
> Yet still I stand by *tilth* and *filth* and *praise*.

Robert Graves had an advantage over most other people in knowing a good many delightful old words, some of the oldest in the language, which have slipped from daily use in the modern world. His appreciation of 'tilth' would no doubt have enabled him to welcome the resurrection of even less familiar words, a selection of which are given here with their definitions.

acclumsid	numbed, paralysed, clumsy
adlubescence	pleasure, delight
agruw	horrify, cause shuddering
bawdreaing	bawdy misbehaviour
brool	low, deep humming, murmur
croodle	creep close, a faint humming, the low music of birds
fadoodle	nonsense, something foolish
flosh	swamp or stagnant pool overgrown with weeds
glop	swallow greedily, stare at in wonder or alarm
gundygut	glutton
hoddypeak	simpleton, blockhead
lennow	flabby, limp
malshave	caterpillar
pingle	eat with little appetite

porknell	one as fat as a pig
ribble	wrinkle, furrow
spuddle	to work feebly or ineffectively
squiddle	waste time with idle talk
ug	fear, dread
vellication	twitching or convulsive movement
widdershins	unlucky, prone to misfortune, the wrong way
wurp	stone's throw, glance of the eye
yurky	itchy
zuche	tree stump

GUESS WHAT

Riddles, either in verse or prose, have entertained the riddlers and the riddled for centuries. Verse riddles became known as enigmas and when Lewis Carroll composed a similar puzzle in 1866 he called it 'Enigma' as well.

You might enjoy working out what Carroll is describing before looking at his 'explication':

I have a large box, two lids, two caps, three established measures, and a great number of articles a carpenter cannot do without. – Then I have always by me a couple of good fish, and a number of a smaller tribe, –besides two lofty trees, fine flowers, and the fruit of an indigenous plant; a handsome stag; two playful animals, and a number of smaller and less tame herd: Also two halls, or places of worship; some weapons of warfare; and many weathercocks: – The steps of an hotel: the House of Commons on the eve of a dissolution; two students or scholars, and some Spanish grandees, to wait upon me.

All pronounce me a wonderful piece of mechanism, but few have numbered up the strange medley of things which compose my whole.

Explication of the Enigma

The whole – is MAN.

The parts are as follows:

A large box – the chest.

Two lids – the eye lids.

Two caps – the knee caps.

Three established measures – the nails, hands, and feet.

A great number of articles a carpenter cannot do without – nails.

A couple of good fish – the soles of the feet.

A number of a smaller tribe – muscles (mussels).

Two lofty trees – the palms (of the hands).

Fine flowers – two lips (tulips), and irises.

The fruit of an indigenous plant – hips.

A handsome stag – the heart (hart).

Two playful animals – the calves.

A number of a smaller and less tame herd – the hairs (hares).

Two halls, or places of worship – the temples.

Some weapons of warfare – the arms, and shoulder blades.

Many weathercocks – the veins (vanes).

The steps of an hotel – the insteps (inn-steps).

The House of Commons on the eve of a Dissolution – the eyes and nose (ayes and noes).

Two students or scholars – the pupils of the eye.

Some Spanish grandees – the tendons (ten dons).

HEADSTRONG AS AN ALLEGORY

Most of us have said them, even if we may not have realized we were uttering a malapropism. And ludicrous misuses of words, particularly through confusion with similar words, have been around for considerably longer than the character in Sheridan's play *The Rivals*, from whom malapropisms take their name.

William Shakespeare gave his constable Dogberry in *Much Ado About Nothing* the same happy knack of verbal confusion, as in this example when he gives evening orders to the Watch:

DOGBERRY: You are thought here to be the most senseless and fit man for the constable of the watch, therefore bear you the lantern. This is your charge: you shall comprehend all vagrom men: you are to bid any man stand, in the prince's name.

WATCH: How, if a' will not stand?

DOGBERRY: Why, then, take no note of him, but let him go: and presently call the rest of the watch together, and thank God you are rid of a knave . . . You shall also make no noise in the streets; for, for the watch to babble and to talk is most tolerable and not to be endured.

Mrs Malaprop first delighted audiences over a century and a half later and, 200 years on, Sheridan's delightful inversions still entertain:

He is the very pine-apple of politeness!

An aspersion upon my parts of speech!

If I reprehend anything in the world, it is the use of my oracular tongue, and a nice derangement of epitaphs!

No caparisons, miss, if you please. Caparisons don't become a young woman.

I own the soft impeachment.

Illiterate him, I say, quite from your memory.

Although the world has moved on from the genteel coterie of *The Rivals* the malapropism is alive and kidding, as you can see:

The English language is going through a resolution.

My father is retarded on a pension.

They had to use biceps to deliver the baby.

No phonographic pictures will be allowed.

My husband is a marvellous lover. He knows all my erroneous zones.

He works in the incinerator where they burn the refuge.

Are you still wearing massacre on your eyes?

He's a wealthy typhoon.

I was so surprised you could have knocked me down with a fender.

HEALTH CONSCIOUS

It has been estimated that in the course of their studies medical students increase their vocabulary by 10,000 words. Mnemonics can play an important part in learning these.

A mnemonic, which may not feature in medical revision but is within the grasp of the layman, is this helpful alphabetical reminder of the value of vitamins:

Vitamin A
Keeps the cold germs away
And tends to make people nervy,
B's what you need
When you're going to seed
And C is specific to scurvy.
Vitamin D makes the bones in your knee
Tough and hard for the service on Sunday,
While E makes hens scratch
And increases the hatch
And brings in more profits on Monday.
Vitamin F never bothers the chef
For this vitamin never existed.
G puts the fight in the old appetite
And you eat all the foods that are listed.
So now when you dine remember these lines:
If long on this globe you will tarry
Just try to be good and pick out more food
From the orchard, the garden, and dairy.

HOLY WRIT

In 1818 a rather extraordinary book was published, with the title of *Introduction to the Critical Study and Knowledge of the Holy Scriptures*. For the author, a theologian named Thomas Hartwell Horne, this was the culmination of a letter-by-letter analysis of the whole of the King James Version of the Bible.

According to his research Dr Horne calculated that the Bible contains 774,746 words (593,493 in the Old Testament and 181,253 in the New Testament), with a total letter count of 3,566,480 letters (2,728,100 in the Old Testament and 838,380 in the New Testament).

He also threw up some lesser known facts about the Bible. The shortest verse is just two words long 'Jesus wept', which constitutes John 11:35. By contrast verse 9 of the eighth chapter of the Book of Esther ranks as the longest verse with its ninety-word description of the Persian Empire. The Book of Esther is the only book in the Bible in which God's name is not mentioned.

His meticulous study had its lighter moments. Imagine the sense of joy at discovering that the twenty-first verse of the seventh chapter of the Book of Ezra contains every letter in the English alphabet except J:

And I, *even* I Artaxerxes the king, do make a decree to all the treasures which are beyond the river, that whatsoever Ezra the priest, the scribe of the law of the God of heaven, shall require of you, it be done speedily.

Readers of Dr Horne's work also discovered that Ezra had some other surprises in store. The opening verses of Ezra are the same as the last two verses of 2 Chronicles which immediately precede them:

Now in the first year of Cyrus king of Persia, that the word of the LORD by the mouth of Jeremiah might be fulfilled, the Lord stirred up the spirit of Cyrus king of Persia, that he made a proclamation throughout all his kingdom, and *put it* also in writing, saying,
2 Thus saith Cyrus king of Persia, The LORD GOD of heaven hath given me all the kingdoms of the earth; and he hath charged me to build him an house at Jerusalem, which *is* in Judah.

Anyone reading Nehemiah, which follows Ezra, must notice something familiar when reading chapter 7. This is a register of those who came from Babylon and repeats almost word for word the second chapter of Ezra which appears a few pages earlier.

I'LL BE WITH YOU –

Alan F G Lewis, the world's greatest punster, has turned the pun into a literary form of great style and polish.

'I'll be with you –' represents just one of his punning formulas:

> I'll be with you –
> in two shakes, said the freemason
> in an instant, said the marketing man
> in two sex, said the hermaphrodite
> in a trice, said the Third Man
> in a flash, said the magician
> in half a tick, said the vivisectionist
> in half a mho, said the electrician
> in necks to no time, said the executioner
> in a twinkling, eye said.

INCLUDE ME OUT

'Include me out' is probably the most celebrated example of Sam Goldwyn's rare command and use of the English language.

Goldwynisms have passed into the language as square pegs in round holes, statements that manage to make sense and nonsense at the same time.

No one can deny Goldwyn's winning formula in the movie industry but his memorable use of English is sure to give as much pleasure as his films far into the future.

To give a flavour of his verbal virtuosity, here are some choice examples:

We're overpaying him, but he's worth it.

We want a story that starts with an earthquake and works its way up to a climax.

Tell me, how do you love my picture?

It's more than magnificent – it's mediocre.

If Roosevelt were alive, he'd turn in his grave.

In two words: im-possible.

I read part of it all the way through.

Let's have some new clichés.

A bachelor's life is no life for a single man.

Anybody who goes to see a psychiatrist ought to have his head examined.

Every director bites the hand that lays the golden egg.

A verbal contract isn't worth the paper it's written on.

We have all passed a lot of water since then.

I'll give you a definite maybe.

Yes, my wife's hands are very beautiful. I'm going to have a bust made of them.

Going to call him William? What kind of name is that? Every Tom, Dick and Harry's called William. Why don't you call him Bill?

Chaplin is no businessman – all he knows is that he can't take anything less.

You ought to take the bull by the teeth.

Gentlemen, I want you to know that I am not always right, but I am never wrong.

If you cannot give me your word of honour will you give me your promise?

A wide screen just makes a bad film twice as bad.

My Toujours Lautrec!

The reason why so many people turned up at Louis B Mayer's funeral was they wanted to make sure he was dead.

I SAY, I SAY, I SAY

Some of the most groan-provoking puns (and some of the most enduring) are those that take the form of the popular 'I say, I say, I say' music-
hall jokes. Those centring round words beginning with J are particular
favourites:

I say, I say, I say – my wife's just gone to the Far East.

Jakarta?

No, she went of her own accord.

I say, I say, I say – my wife's just auditioned for *Oedipus*.

Jocasta?

No, she was terrible.

I say, I say, I say – I've just been picking strawberries with the girl in
the low-cut T-shirt.

Juicy?

Yes, but only when she bent down.

I say, I say, I say – my wife's just been to the Caribbean for a holiday.

Jamaica?

No, she was only too glad to go.

IT'S A SQUARE WORD

Word squares, arrangements of words of equal length that can be read vertically as well as horizontally, have been a source of fascination and entertainment in many languages for thousands of years.

The most frequently quoted ancient example in this country dates from the Roman occupation of Britain. During excavations at a villa near Cirencester archaeologists uncovered this agricultural word square which says a lot about the demands of the rural economy two thousand years ago:

```
R O T A S
O P E R A
T E N E T
A R E P O
S A T O R
```

This forms a Latin sentence which translated into English means 'Arepo the sower controls the wheels with an effort'. This word square has the additional merit of being palindromic: you can read the five words backward or upward, as well as from left to right and downwards. Try it.

Word squares up to five letters long are comparatively straightforward.

One-letter word square: I

Two-letter word square:
```
T O
O N
```

Three-letter word square:
```
T A N
A R E
N E T
```

Four-letter word square:

```
O P A L
P I N E
A N O N
L E N S
```

Five-letter word square :

```
S T U N G
T E N O R
U N T I E
N O I S E
G R E E T
```

Beyond six letters things become more difficult, but not impossible for the experienced word manipulator:

Six-letter word square:

```
E S T A T E
S H A V E N
T A L E N T
A V E R S E
T E N S E R
E N T E R S
```

Seven-letter word square:

```
P R E P A R E
R E M O D E L
E M U L A T E
P O L E M I C
A D A M A N T
R E T I N U E
E L E C T E D
```

Eight-letter word square:

```
A G A R I C U S
G E N E R A N T
A N A C O N D A
R E C A N T E R
I R O N W O R T
C A N T O N A L
U N D E R A G E
S T A R T L E D
```

To create word squares of longer letters requires the use of even more obscure words and place names but, to show that it can be done, here is an example of a nine-letter word square:

```
A N G E L S H I P
N O O N E T I D E
G O L D V I L L E
E N D W E L L E R
L E V E L L I N E
S T I L L E N E S
H I L L I N E S S
I D L E N E S S E
P E E R E S S E S
```

To provide some encouragement, you might like to know that according to Darryl Francis and Dmitri Borgmann, the world's leading authorities on word squares, 900 nine-letter word squares can be constructed!

JOIN THE CLUB

I don't know what the collective noun is for television presenters and I'm not sure that I really need to know what it might be, judging by some of the more bizarre collectives applied to other creatures – how about 'a smarm of gameshow hosts' and 'an arrogance of TV producers'? Fifty of the most evocative and unusual collectives are given here. How many did you know before you looked at the list?

A colony of ANTS

An shrewdness of APES

A cete of BADGERS

A sloth of BEARS

A army of CATERPILLARS

A clowder of CATS

A drove of CATTLE

A peep of CHICKENS

A murder of CROWS

A dule of DOVES

A balding of DUCKS

A school of FISH

A sulk of FOXES

A gaggle of GEESE

A husk of HARES

A cast of HAWKS

A brood of HENS

A siege of HERONS

A harass of HORSES

A smack of JELLYFISH

A kindle of KITTENS

A covey of PARTRIDGE

An ostentation of PEACOCKS

A congregation of PLOVERS

A string of PONIES

A nest of RABBITS

An unkindness of RAVENS

A crash of RHINOCEROSES

A building of ROOKS

A pod of SEALS

A host of SPARROWS

A dray of SQUIRRELS

A murmuration of STARLINGS

A mustering of STORKS

A flight of SWALLOWS

A knot of TOADS

A hover of TROUT

A rafter of TURKEYS

A pitying of TURTLEDOVES

A bale of TURTLES

A gam of WHALES

A rout of WOLVES

A descent of WOODPECKERS

KEEP IT SHORT

Sir Arthur Conan Doyle used to claim that he once sent the same message by telegram to a dozen distinguished men. It read:

ALL IS DISCOVERED. FLY AT ONCE.

According to Conan Doyle all twelve had fled the country within twenty-four hours.

Now that the telegram has gone the same way as the smoke signal and the carrier pigeon, the world of words has lost one of its most resourceful and entertaining means of expression. Fax messages may be instantaneous but they lack the drama and mystery of the telegram. To celebrate its departure here is a selection of the briefest but most telling telegrams to savour and enjoy.

G K Chesterton's wife once received this famous enquiry from her husband:

AM IN MARKET HARBOROUGH. WHERE OUGHT I TO BE?

to which she returned the message:

HOME.

When Gertrude Lawrence married Richard Aldrich her wedding-day messages included this:

DEAR MRS A, HOORAY HOORAY
AT LAST YOU ARE DEFLOWERED.
ON THIS AS EVERY OTHER DAY
I LOVE YOU. NOËL COWARD.

Thomas Mann's daughter, Erika, labelled as an enemy by Hitler's Third Reich, needed a British passport to escape Germany in a hurry. She wrote to W H Auden asking if he would marry her.

The couple had never met, but Auden wired back:

DELIGHTED.

The editor of a magazine, keen to verify copy, sent a telegram to Cary Grant's agent:

HOW OLD CARY GRANT?

The star replied in person:

OLD CARY GRANT FINE. HOW YOU?

During a performance of Of Thee I Sing, Bill Gaxton, one of the cast, received this telegram from the playwright George S Kaufman:

WATCHING YOUR PERFORMANCE FROM LAST ROW. WISH YOU WERE HERE.

Kaufman's friend and fellow writer Robert Benchley sent a telegram to the New Yorker from Venice:

STREETS FULL OF WATER. PLEASE ADVISE.

Noël Coward, taken ill in Italy on one occasion, telegrammed his friend Cole Lesley from Florence:

HAVE MOVED HOTEL EXCELSIOR COUGHING MYSELF INTO A FIRENZE.

When a group of Oxford undergraduates found out that Rudyard Kipling earned ten shillings for every word he wrote they posted him ten shillings asking for one of his very best words in reply. Back came a telegram from Kipling reading:

THANKS.

KEYBOARD CAPERS

Since 1872 English language typewriters have adopted the QWERTY keyboard (named after the first six letters on the top row). QWERTY was developed when the typewriter was in its infancy and inclined to jam if the keys were operated too quickly. The solution at the time seemed to be placing the letters and combinations of letters which appeared most frequently in English as far away from each other as possible. QWERTY came into being and QWERTY is still with us in spite of over a century of advances in communications technology.

Attempts have been made to devise alternative arrangements of letters but none of these have yet broken QWERTY's hold on the keyboard despite its limitations. According to informed estimates, learning to type with QWERTY takes twice as long as it should and makes the typist work twenty times harder than necessary. It would appear that poor old QWERTY doesn't have much to commend it!

From a word puzzler's point of view QWERTY does have one merit. Try forming words in 'typewriter order' and you'll discover it can be quite a challenge. Here is the QWERTY keyboard in full to remind you:

Q W E R T Y U I O P
A S D F G H J K L
Z X C V B N M

Words like, 'tip', 'ask, 'rub' and 'pan' occur in 'typewriter order'. What longer words can you find (double letters are acceptable as in 'tall')? Some examples to inspire you are:

four-letter words: **quip, rush**
five-letter words: **qualm, quill**
seven-letter word: **wettish**

If you restrict yourself to the letters of the top row of the keyboard – QWERTYUIOP – (though not necessarily in that order, you can spell 'quire', 'pepper', and several longer words:

ten-letter words: **typewriter, repertoire, proprietor, perpetuity**
eleven-letter words: **proprietary, rupturewort**

Dropping down to the second row your options are restricted to A S D F G H J K L, which can still produce words like:

five-letter word: **flash**
six-letter word: **flasks**
eight-letters words: **flagfall, haggadah**

KNIT-WIT

One of the regulars in Dictionary Corner during the early days of *Countdown* was my friend Gyles Brandreth, a wit and wordsmith with a fondness for outrageous puns and outlandish knitwear. Viewers would tune in to see what amazing piece of colourful knitwear Gyles was wearing next.

When he gave up *Countdown* for the House of Commons, Gyles was surprised to find that his reputation had preceded him. Speaking in a committee one day, Gyles was interrupted from the Opposition front bench by John Prescott who called out 'Woolly jumper! Woolly jumper!' Gyles continued with his speech and Mr Prescott continued with his barracking, until Gyles paused and pointed out to his heckler that the joy of a woolly jumper is that you can take it off at will, whereas the blight of a woolly mind is that you are lumbered with it for life!

Now that he is an MP Gyles may no longer be playing *Countdown*, but he hasn't lost his love of words nor his enthusiasm for good English. In 1992 he introduced a Private Member's Bill designed to encourage the use of plain language in commercial contracts. This is what he had to say:

Language is what distinguishes the human race: it is the characteristic that sets us apart and makes us unique. Even I, as an ardent animal lover, must acknowledge that, however eloquently a dog may bark, he cannot tell you that his parents were poor but honest. Language makes us unique – and we in this country are born with the privilege of having a unique language as our parent tongue – English, the richest language in the history of humanity.

Our language is rich precisely because it is not pure. Emerson called it 'the sea which receives tributaries from every region under heaven.' It is the language of Chaucer and the King James Bible; of Keats, Joyce, Anthony Trollope and Anthony Burgess. It has taken 2,000 years to reach this far – and where is it now, in 1992? Let me show you, Madam Speaker, by quoting from the terms of sale offered by a certain excellent builders' merchant:

'If and to the extent that any person by whom the Seller has been supplied with the goods supplied hereunder (hereinafter referred to as "the Supplier") validly excludes, restricts or limits his liability to the Seller in respect of the said goods or of any loss or damage arising in connection therewith the liability of the Seller to the Buyer in respect of the said goods or of any loss or damage arising in connection therewith shall be correspondingly excluded restricted or limited.'

There you have it, Madam Speaker: the English language today – and those were just five of more than 100 such lines that feature on the back of the delivery note. When the driver drops off the breeze block and says, 'Sign here, guv', what I have just read out constitutes 5 per cent of what the recipient is agreeing to – whether he likes it or not, and whether he understands it or not.

Does it matter? Yes, I believe that it does. It cannot be good that people regularly sign contracts that they do not understand, and, indeed, are not meant to understand . . .

Costly mistakes can be made. A constituent of mine discovered that when he signed an incomprehensible contract to lease a photo-copier. When he wanted to change the photocopier, he was faced with the option of a so-called settlement charge of about £10,000, which was three times the value of the original equipment, or the prospect of leasing the equipment, whose lifetime according to the manufacturer was three years, for a total of seven years. None of that was clear from the contract whose wording was deliberately obfuscatory and arcane.

The Bill is designed to encourage the use of clear, plain language in commercial contracts and to prevent the unscrupulous, arrogant or incompetent from hiding behind legalese, jargon, gobbledygook or small print. It would apply to consumer contracts, consumer credit contracts – think of all the confusion that we would all be spared if we understood the small print that comes with our credit card – and housing contracts.

The plain language that I have in mind is not so much the language of Shakespeare as that of Dickens, not William Shakespeare but Geoffrey Dickens – clear, no-nonsense language that says what it means and means what it says, language that is indeed a lean, mean fighting machine.

A plain language law might appear to be a contradiction in terms because is it not the law and lawyers which are responsible for much of the gobbledygook found in contracts? I believe I am right in saying that in 1595 an English Chancellor chose to make an example of a particularly wordy document filed in his court. He ordered a hole to be cut in the centre of the document – all 120 pages of it – and had the author's head stuffed through it. The offender was then led around Westminster hall, 100 yards from where we are now – even 100 metres – as an example to all and sundry. Alas, that Elizabethan lesson did not stick; and that is where I come in, four centuries later but not a moment too soon.

I propose that the contracts covered by the Bill should be written in clear and readily understandable language using words with common and everyday meanings, be arranged in a logical order, be suitably divided into paragraphs and headings, be clearly laid out and be easily legible.

It is not asking much, but you, Madam Speaker, might well ask 'Why do people sign contracts they don't understand?' Often it is because they are in no position to negotiate. Most consumer contracts are in standard form, drawn up by the supplier and offered on a take-it-or-leave it basis. The Bill would help consumers. It would also help businesses because those which have taken voluntary steps in the right direction have learnt that clear contracts have advantages and that intelligible contracts promote customers' trust and loyalty and encourage consumers to stick to their contracts. They also achieve savings in management and staff time. The new law would encourage better practice and, if necessary, would enforce it, although the sanctions that I propose are moderate.

The experience in the United States is that a plain language law such as this would immediately improve practice and standards but, if a contract did not comply with the Act, the party which made the contract in the course of business would be liable to an action for damages brought by the other party – so there is also something in this for the lawyers.

That said, there is no question of any form of criminal penalty. Offending contracts would not be void, unenforceable or voidable, I propose compensation for the consumer who can show actual loss and, in some cases, a small sum of additional damages. I also propose, as back-up, an extension of the existing powers of the Director General of Fair Trading to deal directly with businesses which ignore the new law.

The case for such a law is overwhelming. Clear, coherent, easy-to-read consumer contracts bring advantages to consumers and to business, but the signs of voluntary implementation are piecemeal. I believe that, as in the United States, the chief merit of the new law would be its impetus for change. Alas, only legislation will prompt businesses to sit up and start to take notice of their own paperwork.

I trust that the advantages of the Bill will be obvious to the House. Inevitably, some people will not see its virtues, but then, as the saying has it, a slight inclination of the cranium is as adequate as a spasmodic movement of one optic to an equine quadruped utterly devoid of visionary capacity.

LETTER LINE

Questions tailor-made for *Countdown* followers feature in this line-up. All the questions are about letters and all the answers are on page 157:

1   Can you think of a powerful nine-letter English word that contains just one vowel?

2   Can you think of a seven-letter word that doesn't include any of the five vowels?

3   Can you think of a common fifteen-letter word that has one vowel which is repeated five times and no other vowels at all?

4   Two eight-letter words each contain the first six letters of the alphabet. What words are they?

5   Two seventeen-letter words contain the same seventeen letters. What are they?

6   Can you think of two fifteen-letter words that contains all the vowels but in which no letter is used more than once?

7   Which sixteen-letter everyday English word makes repeated use of just one vowel?

8   One word concerned with a great deal of anxiety has fifteen letters which, when it is printed, has no letters that stick up like 'd' and none that stick down like 'g'?

9   Which English word has the letter I six times and no other vowel?

10 Which English word contains three sets of twin letters, each pair coming directly after the one before?

LETTERS PLAY

The long-running success of *Countdown* confirms that alphabet word play is a well-established favourite. Poets have amused themselves writing A–Z verses that each start with the next letter of the alphabet.

The popular children's rhyme is a typical example:

A was apple-pie;

B bit it,

C cut it,

D dealt it,

E eat it,

F fought for it,

G got it,

H had it,

I inspected it,

J jumped for it,

K kept it,

L longed for it,

M mourned for it,

N nodded at it,

O opened it,

P peppered it,

Q quartered it,

R ran for it,

S stole it,

T took it,

U upset it,

V viewed it,

W wanted it,

X, Y, Z, and ampersand

All wished for a piece in the hand.

More ambitious was the 'Siege of Belgrade', a masterpiece of invention which manages to combine the alphabet (excepting the letter J) with alliteration to produce a poem of remarkable, if questionable, consistency:

An Austrian army awfully array'd,
Boldly by battery besieg'd Belgrade:
Cossack commanders cannonading come,
Dealing destruction's devastating doom.
Every endeavour engineers essay –
For fame, for fortune fighting – furious fray!
Generals 'gainst generals grapple – gracious God!
How honours Heav'n heroic hardihood –
Infuriate – indiscriminate in ill,
Kinsmen kill kindred, kindred kinsmen kill.
Labour low levels longest, loftiest lines –
Men march 'mid mounds, 'mid moles, 'mid murd'rous mines.
Now noisy noxious numbers notice naught,
Of outward obstacles opposing ought;
Poor patriots! partly purchas'd, partly press'd,
Quite quaking quickly, 'quarter, quarter,' quest.
Reason returns, religious right redounds,
Suwarrow stops such sanguinary sounds.
Truce to thee, Turkey, triumph to thy train,
Unjust, unwise, unmerciful Ukraine,
Vanish vain vict'ry, vanish vict'ry vain.
Why wish we warfare? wherefore welcome were
Xerxes, Ximenes, Xanthus, Xaviere?
Yield, yield, ye youths, yeomen yield your yell;
Zeno's, Zorpater's, Zoroaster's, zeal
Attracting all, arms against acts appeal.

LOSS LEADERS

Word games in which letters are removed may be at odds with the aim of *Countdown*, but they call for just as much ingenuity on the part of the players.

Beheadments is a game in which letters are removed from the beginning of a word, so that each time a letter is removed the remaining letters also spell a word, an example is the word 'class', which can be beheaded to make: 'lass' and 'ass'.

The same principle has been turned to an elegant use in poetry. George Herbert's poem 'Paradise', written in the first half of the seventeenth century, removes the opening letters from the final words in a number of verses:

> I blesse thee, Lord, because I GROW
> Among thy trees, which in ROW
> To thee both fruit and order OW
>
> What open force, or hidden CHARM
> Can blast my fruit, or bring me HARM
> While the inclosure is thine ARM?
>
> Inclose me still for fear I START.
> Be to me rather sharp and TART,
> Then let me want thy hand and ART
>
> When thou dost greater judgements SPARE,
> And with thy knife but prune and PARE
> Ev'n fruitful trees more fruitful ARE.
> Such sharpness shows the sweetest FREND:
> Such cuttings rather heal than REND:
> And such beginnings touch their END.

MAP REFERENCE

Hiding the names of countries inside sentences and then asking someone else to find them has been a popular word game for many years. It may sound simple, but you have to develop an eye for the game to discover what you're looking for quickly. For example the names of two countries, Malta and India, are hidden in the sentence, 'Have you heard an animal talk in dialect?'

It's fun devising sentences of your own, and to give a feel for what's involved try your knowledge of geography on these, each of which includes two hidden countries (answers are on pages 157–8):

1 Such a display could be either grand or rather vulgar.

2 In December mud and slush surround the fine palace.

3 Vladimir and Olga are Soviet names.

4 Children put on galoshes to go out in the rain.

5 Give a dog a bone and give him a little water.

6 If your exhaust pipe rusts you just have to shrug and accept it.

7 Interpol and the FBI discover hidden marksmen.

8 Evening classes may help an amateur to improve his painting.

MEASURING UP

When it comes to using and understanding measurements most of us get by with an everyday mix of units: litres, grams, centimetres, metres, miles, pints, degrees Celsius (and Fahrenheit), inches, yards, volts and watts.

For the specialist in different fields of scientific work and commerce the vocabulary of metrology is considerably richer. Here are two dozen units and, in random order, the uses to which they are put. See how many you can match correctly (answers on page 158)

angstrom	electric conductance
becquerel	amount of substance containing as many elementary entities as there are atoms in 0.012kg of carbon-12
cable	plane angle between two radii of a circle
coulomb	radiation absorbed dose
farad	force
gray	electric resistance
henry	magnetic flux
hertz	work, energy, quantity of heat
jeroboam	electric capacitance
joule	electric charge
kelvin	one hundred-millionth of a centimetre
link	inductance
mole	magnetic flux density
nebuchadnezzar	216 gallons
newton	frequency
ohm	4 bottles of champagne
pascal	24 sheets of paper
peck	thermodynamic temperature
quire	7.92 inches
radian	240 yards
siemens	2 gallons
tesla	pressure, stress
tun	radiation activity
weber	20 bottles of champagne

MILITARY INTELLIGENCE

'Military intelligence' is a popular example of an oxymoron, a combination of apparent contradictions originally used as a rhetorical device and now bandied about without too much thought at all.

Collecting oxymorons is fun and develops your feel for language use and abuse.

When they are correctly used oxymorons can be arresting; Tennyson's lines from 'Lancelot and Elaine' are frequently quoted examples:

> His honour rooted in dishonour stood,
> And faithful unfaithful kept him falsely true.

When they crop up unintentionally the results are often amusing. Adverbs are prime culprits when they are used in expressions like 'terribly pleased' and 'immensely small'.

Others frequently pass through the language unnoticed by all but the oxymoron-hunter. In politics the eagle-eyed have picked up: 'Progressive Conservatives' (a Canadian political party) and 'peerless House of Lords'. 'Left-wing fascism' is not unheard of.

Oxymorons can be unforgiving, whoever referred to a Belgian celebrity might have paused for reflection.

METAPHORICALLY
SPEAKING

No one need feel abashed about mixing metaphors. William Shakespeare wasn't above giving Hamlet a celebrated example in his famous 'To be, or not to be' soliloquy, when he wrote the words 'to take arms against a sea of troubles'.

Mixed metaphors frequently go unnoticed. 'Galloping inflation', 'hogging the limelight', 'latching on to a new craze' are typical examples. Only a metaphor mixed with another to produce an incongruous image catches our attention. Noteworthy examples are:

Wild horses on their bended knees would not make me do it.

All these whited sepulchres are tarred with the same brush.

It is the thin end of the white elephant.

The whole chain of events consists entirely of missing links.

He is a rough diamond with a heart of gold.

The views of the grass roots are not hearing the light of day.

The sacred cows have come home to roost with a vengeance.

There is no head of steam to which one can harness oneself.

We're not out of the woods yet by a long chalk.

Politicians are no strangers to mixed metaphors and one of the most famous comes from the eighteenth-century Irish politician Sir Boyle Roche who announced in the House of Commons:

Mr Speaker, I smell a rat; I see him forming in the air and darkening the sky; but I'll nip him in the bud.

MISSING THE TOWN DRAIN

Fate may have been less than even-handed with the Reverend William Archibald Spooner, sometime Dean and later Warden of New College, Oxford. Today the kindly, hospitable don is remembered for the metahesis from which he was supposed to suffer.

The what?

Metahesis – the tendency to transpose initial letters or half-syllables often with amusing consequences. But we don't call them metaheses, 'spoonerism' fits the bill so much better.

It's doubtful whether Spooner was responsible for any of the classic spoonerisms and he certainly wasn't responsible for the number that bear his name. Throughout his life he suffered from weak eyesight which gave him a hesitant, slightly nervous disposition. These mannerisms of an absent-minded professor were ideally suited to one credited with announcing a hymn in the college chapel as 'Kinquering kongs their titles take', which is thought of as the original spoonerism.

Adroit turns of phrase like 'I remember your name. I just can t think of your face' and 'Tell me, was it you or your brother who was killed in the war?' fuelled the myth. Before long Spooner's name was associated with many a well-crafted and carefully polished 'slip of the tongue'.

Undergraduates were censored:

You have tasted a whole worm.

You will leave Oxford on the next town drain.

You have hissed all my mystery lectures.

You were fighting a liar in the quad.

Fellow members of the Senior Common Room were bemused:

Is the bean dizzy?

Let us toast our queer old dean.

I have just received a blushing crow.

Members of the chapel congregation were nonplussed:

Excuse me, madam, you appear to be occupewing my pie.

Allow me to sew you into another sheet.

The Lord is a shoving leopard.

Warden Spooner died in 1930 but not before the English language had set off in pursuit of the verbal slips that will always be associated with him.

MIX ME A METAGRAM

Metagrams are riddles formed by changing the first letter of a particular word again and again to produce as many words as possible of different meanings.

A fairly simple metagram is one based on three-letter words like this:

> Well known to all as a covering for the head;
> Change my initial, a doze I mean instead.
> Once more, and an opening you will see;
> Exchange again, I'm found inside a tree.
> Once more, I mean then to befall.
> Again, I'm used by travellers, one and all.
> Again, in this my mother often nursed me.
> Exchange again. and this my food would be.
> Again, and a sharp blow you've spelled.
> Once more, and a blow that's hardly seen or felt.

The words created are: cap, nap, gap, sap, hap, map, lap, pap, rap and tap.

For a slightly longer one try this:

> Of letters four, I do denote
> A man of wisdom great,
> But cooks do often me devote
> To share – alas! – a goose's fate;
> But change my head and then, instead,
> Part of a book you'll find;
> And if again I'm carefully read,
> A youth who walks behind;
> Change once again, and then you will
> A furious passion see,
> Which reason vainly tries to still,
> Keep far removed from me;
> Another change, and you will then
> See I'm remuneration
> Earned by all grades of working men
> Throughout the British nation;

But change my head once more, and then
A prison I appear.
From which sweet sounds oft issue forth
That pleasant are to hear.

The words in this are: sage, page, rage, wage and cage.

In this example the metagrammist is kind enough to tell you which letters you should be using, though this in no way diminishes his artistry:

There's a word, you'll agree, commencing with B
That expresses a cool pleasant shade;
But remove letter B and substitute C,
Apprehensively shrinking is made;
Take away letter C, replace it by D,
It will name what's bestowed on a bride;
Now if D is erased and by G replaced,
A Welsh word, meaning crooked is spied;
Thus far very well, now substitute L,
We are going down now you will say;
Letter L shall be gone, and M be put on,
There's a man cutting grass to make hay;
But when M shall have fled put P there instead,
It will name what is mentioned of steam;
Pray just now P erase, put R in its place,
There's a man gliding down with the stream;
But now take R away, put S there, we say,
That a farmer at work then it names;
If for S you put T you surely will name
A noted place close by the Thames.

NO TWO ALIKE

A few years ago the Today programme on Radio 4 ran a very successful mini-saga competition. Contestants composed tales of exactly 100 words, the best of which were read on the programme and later published in an anthology.

Following even sterner restrictions, students at an American high school were challenged to write a 100-word composition in which no word was repeated. They put their heads together and came up with this:

Let's Go! The challenge is to write a composition without using any word more than once. Do you think it can be done? If not, give one reason for doing this. While we are sitting here in English class at Pompton Lakes High School, Lakeside Avenue, New Jersey, all of us figure out something which makes sense. Mrs Feldman helps her pupils because another teacher said they couldn't accomplish such tasks. Nobody has fresh ideas right now. Goal – 100! How far did students get? Eighty-five done already; fifteen left. 'Pretty soon none!' says Dennis O'Neill. Gary Putnam and Debra Petsu agree. So there!

ONE AND ONLY

H E Dudeney, who died sixty-five years ago, was England's greatest creator of puzzles.

One of his most appealing was this superficially simple crossword. At a glance the grid looks straightforward, it's when you find out that each of the twenty-six letters of the alphabet is used once and once only that it starts to appear more complex. Then come the definitions, a few of which are rather obscure. Lastly, there are the solutions which the solver must work out and then fit into the grid because Dudeney gives no clues as to what fits where or in which direction!

You will find the solution on page 159.

Definitions

A metal. Parts of trees. To annoy.
Whim or Imagination. A sign,
example. What person or persons.
A man's shortened Christian name.
To puzzle or, make sport of.

ONE-STOP VERSE

James Joyce and William Faulkner are two of the many writers who have written extended passages without the use of punctuation. Whether or not these rank as sentences in the purely grammatical sense is questionable. Marcel Proust wrote a sentence 958 words long in *Cities of the Plain*. In English the prize for the longest sentence goes to one in Sylvester Hassell's *History of the Church of God* which runs to 3,153 words.

These monsters are all in prose of course. Long verse sentences are less common but John Slim's 'Death Sentence' shows what can be achieved when a poet sets mind and muse to the task.

Death Sentence

Have you heard how Cuthbert Hatch
To find a gas leak, struck a match
And thereby hastened his despatch
To realms unknown to you and me,
Who have not yet been foolishly
Inclined to leave posterity
To puzzle for itself just why
We chose to make our fragments fly
For ever upwards to the sky,
As Cuthbert did when in the dark
He smelled a smell and sparked a spark
Which sent him rising like a lark
 – A very shattered fowl, it's true,
With no lump large enough to stew
And nothing any cat could chew –
Into unresisting space
Where there is never any place
To rest one's feet or wash one's face,
Though this, for faceless, feetless folk,
As Cuthbert was by then, poor bloke,
Is not by any means a yoke
Which is impossible to bear,
For it's with truth that I declare
That cases are extremely rare

Of people ceasing to exist
And then, assuming they'll be missed,
Proceeding forthwith to insist
On spreading sadness with their pen
Among their former fellow-men
With news of things beyond their ken
By writing letters to the Press
To say that they are in a mess
Which words in print cannot express,
For they're aware that we below
Quite rarely care just how they go
And, once they've gone, don't want to know
The finer details of the fate
Which suddenly transformed their state
From Man Alive into The Late
Lamented such as Cuthbert Hatch,
Who found that leak with lighted match
And who thereafter failed to catch
The interest of the public eye
Or stir mankind to spare a sigh
Which may explain precisely why
I think that Cuthbert Hatch (The Late)
Would not expect to read (or rate)
A second sentence on his fate?

ONLY Q

Just as we grow up to believe I before E except after C, most of us go to our graves believing that Q is always followed by U. As the list below shows this isn't necessarily the case.

English has absorbed many words from other languages where this rule does not apply and all of these words can now be found comfortably ensconced in the pages of a variety of English dictionaries.

qabbala	a mystical interpretation of the Scriptures
qadi	a Muslim judge interpreting and administering Islamic religious law
qaf	the twenty-first letter of the Arabic alphabet
qaid	a local Muslim administrator in Spain or North Africa
qaimaqam	a minor official serving the Ottoman empire
qanat	an underground tunnel used to convey water
qaneh	a Hebrew measurement equalling 10.25 feet
qantar	a unit of weight used around the Mediterranean
qasab	an ancient measure used in Arabia equalling 12.6 feet
qasida	a laudatory or satiric poem in Arabic
qat	an Arabian shrub used as a narcotic
qhat	an obsolete spelling of 'what'
qhwom	an obsolete spelling of 'whom'
qiana	the trade name of a fabric related to nylon
qibia	the point to which Muslims turn to pray
qinah	a Hebrew dirge or lament
qintar	an Albanian unit of money
qobar	a dry fog that forms in the area of the Upper Nile
qvint	a Danish weight

OPPOSITE NUMBERS

Anagrams are amusing when they reflect the meaning of the word or phrase from which they are derived, but they can be even more entertaining when, as antigrams, they take on a contrary meaning, so 'funeral' becomes 'real fun' and 'enormity' is transformed into 'more tiny'.

A few examples might inspire you to create antigrams of your own:

adversaries	are advisers
a picture of health	Oft pale, I ache, hurt
discretion	is no credit
filled	ill-fed
infection	fine tonic
militarism	I limit arms
misfortune	it's more fun
old man winter	warm, indolent
protectionism	nice to imports
the man who laughs	he's glum, won't ha-ha
violence	nice love

ORDER ORDER

Can you think of a word in which the four consecutive letters A B C D appear in the correct order?

There may be other answers but among commonly used words 'abscond' fits the bill. Indeed 'absconded' goes one better with the first five letters A B C D E in the correct order.

It's possible to work through the alphabet with groups of four letters used in order. This is one way:

d e f g	defying
f g h i	fighting
h i j k	hijack
m n o p	monopoly
q r s t	querist
r s t u	understudy
x y z	oxygenize

PIGGY IN THE MIDDLE

We've already looked at words that begin and end with consecutive letters of the alphabet so for a change here are three sets of words in which the middle letters run from A to Z. To add to the fun the letters on either side of these central letters form words as well, three-letter words, four-letter words and five-letter words respectively.

As you'll see the two that have stumped us are the words with Q in the middle.

seven letters	nine letters	eleven letters
carAvan	bungAlows	blockAdings
jawBone	rainBowed	underBought
teaCher	blueCoats	extraCtable
banDits	snowDrift	screwDriver
vetEran	bothEring	adultErated
warFare	goldFinch	satinFlower
bagGage	kiloGrams	underGround
witHout	brigHtens	unrigHtable
ManIkin	handIwork	deterIorate
conJure	flapJacks	interJangle
weeKend	sparKling	underKeeled
lowLand	paneLwork	oversLoping
barMaid	clayMores	blackMailed
furNace	lameNting	heaveNwards
bayOnet	bestOwing	trampOlines
ramPart	tramPling	enterPrises
—	—	—
curRant	mayoRship	butteRflies
penSion	brimStone	sweepStakes
vanTage	sideTrack	forgeTtable
bitUmen	consUlate	prestUdying
canVass	disaVowed	extraVagant
hogWash	bushWomen	lightWeight
ManXman	trioXides	overeXpress
copYcat	pansYlike	staphYlions
manZana	waltZlike	hydraZonium

PSEUDODROMES

Whereas in a palindrome it's the individual letters that read the same forwards and backwards, in a pseudodrome it's whole words. Sentences formed by pseudodromes may not appeal to palindrome purists but they can be every bit as entertaining, as these pseudodromes show:

Bores are people that say that people are bores.

Does milk machinery milk does?

Dollars make men covetous, then covetous men make dollars.

Girl, bathing on Bikini, eyeing boy, finds boy eyeing bikini on bathing girl.

So patient a doctor to doctor a patient so.

Women understand men; few men understand women.

You can cage a swallow, can't you, but you can't swallow a cage, can you?

PUNCTUATION PLEASE

To make sense of this sentence a little punctuation is required. See how long it takes you to supply it. (Answer on page 159.)

THAT THAT IS IS THAT THAT IS NOT IS NOT IS NOT THAT IT IT IS

QUICK BROWN FOX

'A quick brown fox jumps over the lazy dog', the sentence familiar to many when they learned to type is thirty-three letters long and contains every letter of the alphabet; as such it is probably the best-known pangram in English.

Pangrams, or sentences that include every letter of the alphabet, have been testing the ingenuity of writers since long before the typewriter. We will never know whether Shakespeare deliberately set out to produce a pangram in these lines spoken by Coriolanus, but apart from Z he managed to include all twenty-six letters:

> O, a kiss
> Long as my exile, sweet as my revenge!
> Now, by the jealous queen of heaven, that kiss
> I carried from thee, dear, and my true lip
> Hath virgin'd it e'er since.

In the Bible the First Book of Chronicles comes as close in 12:40, missing out by just the letter Q:

Moreover they that were nigh them, *even* unto Issachar and Zebulun and Naphtali, brought bread on asses, and on camels, and on mules, and on oxen, *and* meat, meal, cakes of figs, and bunches of raisins, and wine, and oil, and oxen, and sheep abundantly: for there was joy in Israel.

Shorter pangrams require more licence in the form of proper names and words con veniently borrowed from languages like Hebrew and Welsh.

In descending order of letter-count they include:

32 letters: Pack my box with five dozen liquor jugs.

31 letters: The five boxing wizards jump quickly.

30 letters: How quickly daft jumping zebras vex.

29 letters: Quick wafting zephyrs vex bold Jim.

28 letters: Waltz; nymph for quick jigs vex Bud.

27 letters: Brick quiz whangs jumpy veldt fox.

To produce a pangram with each letter used just once calls for a certain degree of tolerance on the part of the reader. However, 'Frowzy things plumb vex'd Jack Q' fits the bill and doesn't require footnotes to be understood!

READ ME A REBUS

R U good at lateral thinking? If U R U will C how 2 solve these rebuses.

A rebus, in case you haven't rumbled it, is, to give a dictionary definition, 'an enigmatic representation of a name or a word or a phrase by pictures or letters or numbers or other words or phrases'. Anyone who has bought the *Countdown* magazine will know that John Meade, *Countdown's* executive producer/director, is a master of this form of puzzle. Look out for his WORPIX.

Right, it's over to you now – C how U get on with these (answers on page 159):

1   What's this?

> E
> M
> A
> R
> F

2   Why is one of these important every day?

> ME
> A L

3   Can you resolve this?

> ONE ANOTHER
> ONE ANOTHER
> ONE ANOTHER
> ONE ANOTHER
> ONE ANOTHER
> ONE ANOTHER

4   What's unsettled about this?

> WETHER

5   Why would you expect to find meat on this word?

                    B
                    E

6   What play is this?

                              ADO
                  ADO   ADO
        ADO   O   ADO

                  ADO   ADO
                          ADO

REDUNDANT TO REQUIREMENTS

The workplace can be harsh and unrewarding, even in a harmless punning game.

Here are thirty types of employment and the occupational hazards they bring with them. How many more can you add to the list?

Accountants are disfigured.

Admirals are abridged.

Advertisers are declassified.

Bankers are disinterested.

Botanists are deflowered.

Clerks are defiled.

Choristers are unsung.

Committee members are disappointed.

Diplomats are disconsulate.

Electricians are discharged.

Gunsmiths are fired.

Hairdressers are distressed.

Jurors are unsworn.

Lawyers are debriefed.

Mathematicians are nonplussed.

Models are denuded.

Neurologists are unnerved.

Orchestra leaders are disbanded.

Politicians are devoted.

Private eyes are undetected.

Puzzlers are dissolved.

Songwriters are decomposed.

Surveyors are dislocated.

Tailors are unsuited.

Teachers are outclassed.

Tennis players are unloved and defaulted.

Train drivers are derailed.

Tree surgeons are uprooted.

Violinists are unstrung.

Winemakers are deported.

Witch doctors are dispelled.

RESIDENT ALIENS

English belongs to the Indo-European group of languages and naturally the majority of English words are derived from that source. However, there are a considerable number of words from different language groups, many of which have become so well-established that discovering their origins comes as a surprise. An A–Z of twenty-six of these imported words shows what I mean:

Admiral	Arabic	**Nadir**	Arabic
Bamboo	Malay	**Orangutan**	Malay
Chocolate	Nahuatl	**Pariah**	Tamil
Damask	Hebrew	**Quinine**	Quechua
Eskimo	Cree	**Racoon**	Powhatan
Fakir	Arabic	**Shawl**	Persian
Gingham	Malay	**Thug**	Hindi
Hammock	Taino	**Ukulele**	Hawaiian
Igloo	Eskimo	**Voodoo**	Ewe
Jaguar	Guarani	**Wadi**	Arabic
Kowtow	Chinese (Mandarin)	**X**	Arabic
Lemon	Arabic	**Yogurt**	Turkish
Mattress	Arabic	**Zebra**	Kikongo

RHYMING SOLO

For anyone suffering from insomnia, or stuck in a traffic jam or otherwise in need of some mental stimulation, trying to compose a piece of verse using only a single rhyme might be an amusing diversion.

The choice of rhyme is important. End your first verse with 'tiger' for instance and you'll have trouble writing more than a few verses.

A Victorian alphabet verse with a carefully chosen rhyme shows what can be done.

> A was an Army, to settle disputes;
> B was a Bull, not the mildest of brutes;
> C was a Cheque, duly drawn upon Coutts;
> D was King David, with harps and with lutes;
> E was an Emperor, hailed with salutes;
> F was a Funeral, followed by mutes;
> G was a Gallant in Wellington boots;
> H was a Hermit who lived upon roots;
> I was Justinian in his Institutes;
> K was a keeper, who commonly shoots;
> L was a Lemon, the sourest of fruits;
> M was a Ministry – say Lord Bute's;
> N was a Nicholson, famous on flutes;
> O was an Owl, that hisses and hoots;
> P was a Pond, full of leeches and newts;
> Q was a Quaker, in whitey-brown suits;
> R was a Reason, which Paley refutes;
> S was a Sergeant with twenty recruits;
> T was Ten Tories of doubtful reputes;
> U was Uncommonly bad cheroots;
> V Vicious motives, Which malice imputes;
> X an Ex-King driven out by emeutes;
> Y is a Yarn; then, the last rhyme that suits;
> Z is the Zuyder Zee, dwelt in by coots.

RIDDLES AND RHYMES

Riddles and rhymes are popular partners and never more so than with Lewis Carroll who created dozens of rhyming riddles, like this which dates from 1870:

> Three sisters at breakfast were feeding the cat.
> The first gave it sole – Puss was grateful for that.
> The next gave it salmon – which Puss thought a treat.
> The third gave it herring – which Puss wouldn't eat.
> Can you explain the cat's behaviour?

Can you? Lewis Carroll wrote his answer in rhyme for anyone who needed a helping hand:

> That salmon and sole Puss should think very grand
> Is no such remarkable thing.
> For more of these dainties Puss took up her stand;
> But when the third sister stretched out her fair hand,
> Pray why should Puss swallow her ring?

Rhyming riddles are easier to remember than those that don't rhyme, though that doesn't make them any easier to solve. To prove the point, have a go at unriddling these and see how long they take you (answers on page 160):

> 1 In spring I look gay
>   Decked in comely array,
>   In summer more clothing I wear;
>   When colder it grows
>   I fling off my clothes,
>   And in winter quite naked appear.
>   What am I?

> 2 Thirty white horses upon a red hill,
>   Now they champ, now they clamp,
>   And now they stand still.
>   What are they?

3 Little Nancy Etticoat
   In a white petticoat
   And a red nose;
   The longer she stands
   The shorter she grows.
   What is she?

4 Runs smoother than any rhyme,
   Loves to fall but cannot climb.
   What is it?

5 What's in the church, but not in the steeple,
   The parson has it, but not the people.

6 Goes to the door and doesn't knock,
   Goes to the window and doesn't rap,
   Goes to the fire and doesn't warm,
   Goes upstairs and does no harm.
   What is it?

7 Long legs, crooked toes,
   Glassy eyes, snotty nose.
   What is it?

8 A riddle, a riddle, as I suppose;
   A hundred eyes and never a nose.
   What is it?

9 Never sings a melody, never has a song,
   But goes on humming all day long.
   What is it?

10 Riddle me, riddle me, riddle me ree,
   I saw a nutcracker up in a tree.
   What was it?

SALLY SELLS SEASHELLS . . .

'Sally sells seashells by the seashore' is one of the best known English tongue twisters. For speakers of the South African Xhosa language this may be an even sterner test:

Iqaqa laziqikaqika kwaze kwaqhawaka uqhoqhoqha.

In the English translation it reads, 'The skunk rolled and ruptured its larynx.'

There's an equally challenging sentence in Czech with similar anatomical references:

Strch prst skrz krk.

That means 'Stick a finger in the throat'. The Czech version of Countdown would also be interesting – vowels don't appear to have the importance they do in English, if this is anything to go by.

English speakers have plenty to contend with apart from Sally and her marine enterprises. Veterinary practice in Arabia poses this challenge:

The sixth sheik's sixth sheep's sick.

Try saying it quickly a few times and when you have got your tongue round that, have a go at these truly tortuous tongue twisters:

The rat ran by the river with a lump of raw liver.

That bloke's back brake-block broke.

Which wristwatches are Swiss wristwatches?

Mumblings bumblings. Bumblings mumblings.

He ran from the Indies to the Andes in his undies.

Rubber baby buggy bumpers.

Ted threw Fred three free throws.

Six thick thistle sticks.

A lump of red leather, a red leather lump.

Tuesday is stew day. Stew day is Tuesday.

The new nuns knew the true nuns knew the new nuns too.

There are thirty thousand feathers on that thrush's throat.

How much wood would a woodchuck chuck, if a woodchuck would chuck wood?

The gum glew grew glum.

Three free thugs set three thugs free.

A big blue bucket of blue blueberries.

Do drop in at the Dewdrop Inn.

Is there a pleasant peasant present?

Three thrice-freed thieves.

Diligence dismisseth despondency.

SENSE OF PLACE

Proper names are not permitted on *Countdown*, at least they aren't when they are just proper names. However, there are a fair a number of place names alone that lead double lives by passing as perfectly respectable nouns. A couple of dozen examples prove the point:

berlin	a type of carriage	**kent**	knew
boston	a card game	**lima**	a bean
chile	a hot pepper	**limerick**	a humorous verse
china	fine porcelain	**morocco**	a soft leather
etna	a container for heating liquids	**pacific**	peaceful
		scotia	a concave moulding
fulham	a loaded die	**surrey**	a light carriage
geneva	a liquor	**texas**	the uppermost structure on a steamboat
guernsey	a woollen jumper		
harrow	to break up and level soil		
		tripoli	a soft, friable rock
holland	a cotton fabric	**ulster**	a long, loose overcoat
japan	to coat with glossy, black lacquer	**wales**	marks with welts
		yonkers	young gentlemen
jersey	a knitted jumper		

SEXY SHEETS
AND DANISH DANCING

In case you get the wrong idea a 'sexto' is a piece of paper cut six from a sheet and a 'sextur' is a Danish dance for six couples, which goes to show that there is a lot more to the letters SEX than you might first imagine.

To prove the point twenty sex-words appear with their definitions, most, but not all, of which are connected in some way with the number 6:

sexadecimal	relating to 16
sexagenary	based on the number 60
sexagene	multiplied by 60 or a power of 60
sexdigit	person with six fingers
sexdigital	having six fingers
sexen	long fishing boat powered by six oars
sexennarian	six-year-old child
sexennial	occurring every six years
sexennium	a period of six years
sexfid	divided into six segments
sexfoil	having six leaves
sexious	sectarian
sexmillenary	of six thousand years
sextain	stanza of six lines
sextans	bronze coin of the Roman Republic
sexti partition	divisions into sixths
sextile	measured by sixty degrees
sextoncy	the office of sexton
sextuple	six-fold
sexvirate	body of six colleagues

SINGULARLY FISHY

What are the plurals of these fish: chub, cod, trout, salmon, and squid?

They're the same as the singular forms of each of the nouns: chub, cod, trout, salmon and squid. Peculiar, you might think, but the same applies to many animals like sheep and buffalo.

Singular plurals are just some of the difficulties newcomers to the language have to tackle when they start referring to more than one of many things. How could you start to explain these for instance?

brother	brethren	**pince-nez**	pince-nez
englyn	englynion	**plural**	plurals
goosefoot	goosefoots	**riff**	riff
hog	hog	**rubai**	rubaiyat
juger	jugera	**shtetl**	shtetlach
landsman	landsleit	**tenderfoot**	tenderfoots
mongoose	mongooses	**ulcus**	ulcera
never-was	never-weres	**vila**	vily
ornis	ornithes	**wunderkind**	wunderkinder
paries	parieties	**yad**	yadayim

SOUNDS PECULIAR

It's a happy coincidence in English that the sounds of so many letters are echoed in a wide number of words. Certain letters like C and U lend themselves to rebuses, but, with the addition of the word 'for', the scope for creating a comic alphabet is far greater. One example is given below, but there are many variants:

A for —ism

B for lamb

C for miles

D for mation

E for brick

F for 'tlass

G for police

H for consent

I for the engine

J for hear such a thing

K for another cup of tea

L for leather

M for size

N for cement

O for the moon

P for Ming seals

Q for tickets

R for minute

S for you

T for two

U for me

V for voce

W for quits

X for X for . . . read all about it

Y for runts

Z for us did softly play

SUFFICIENCIES
AND DEFICIENCIES

One of the things you learn about the English language from working on a programme like *Countdown* is that many of the rules about spelling you learnt at school aren't reflected in the dictionary. 'Sufficiencies' and 'deficiences' are contradictions of one of the best known rules 'I before E except after C'. They each break the rule twice!

English is dotted with words in which an E comes before an I without there being a E in sight and in which an I comes before an E immediately after a C.

Take a look at these examples to prove the point:

ageism	heifer	reindeer
ancient	heir	science
being	inveigle	seize
caffeine	leisure	skein
conscience	mercies	sleigh
deign	neighbour	sovereign
eighth	neither	species
fancied	obeisance	tenancies
feint	plebeian	their
financier	policies	veiled
foreign	proficient	vein
freight	reign	weigh
glacier	reimburse	weir

116

TAKE A LETTER

Take a letter. Add another letter to form a word. Now add a third letter to form a three-letter word and repeat the process, adding a letter a time to make a new word. The process is easy. The challenge is how far can you go until you run out of letters to make words.

With practice you'd be surprised how many words can form, as these examples show. Potential *Countdown* contestants take note!

a	the first letter of the alphabet
an	the indefinite article
ang	the hairy part of an ear of barley
ange	trouble, affliction, anguish
angel	a celestial spirit
angeli	town in Finland
angelic	having the nature of an angel
angelica	aromatic plant used in cooking
angelical	having the nature of an angel
angelicals	nuns of an extinct order founded in Milan in 1530
b	the second letter of the alphabet
bi	bisexual
bit	a piece
bitt	a post on a ship's deck
bitte	spelling of 'bitt' used in the fourteenth, fifteenth and sixteenth centuries
bitter	sharp
bittern	any of various small and medium-sized herons
bitterne	a seventeenth-century spelling of 'bittern'
bitternes	the plural of bitterne
bitterness	the quality of being bitter

bitternesse	an old spelling of bitterness
bitternesses	the plural of bitterness

You can play this game in reverse by placing the new letter in front of the first and so on:

e	the fifth letter of the alphabet
te	a musical note
ate	the past tense of 'eat'
rate	a charge, payment, or price
irate	angry
pirate	a robber on the high seas
spirate	voiceless
aspirate	to pronounce with an H sound

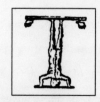

TAKING UP REFERENCES

'If you can get this man to work for you, you will be very fortunate' – that is what most of us would regard as a typically ambiguous employment reference. The great French statesman Cardinal Richelieu is credited with the altogether more accomplished testimony which follows. Whether or not Richelieu actually wrote this masterpiece of ambiguity, it does reflect the qualities of statesmanship and intrigue that made him famous. It is also a splendid example of an equivoque, a composition (usually a verse) which can be read in two different ways.

To appreciate Richelieu's reference the letter should first be read across, then mentally folded in the middle and the first column read alone.

Sir, Mons Compigne, a Savoyard by birth, a Friar of the order of Saint Benedict, is the man who will present to you as his passport to your protection, this letter. He is one of the most discreet, the wisest and the least meddling persons that I have ever known or have had the pleasure to converse with. He has long earnestly solicited me to write to you in his favour, and to give him a suitable character, together with a letter of credence; which I have accordingly granted to his real merit, rather I must say, than to his importunity; for, believe me, Sir, his modesty is only exceeded by his worth. I should be sorry that you should be wanting in serving him on account of being misinformed of his real character; I should be afflicted if you were as some other gentlemen have been, misled on that score, who now esteem him, and those among the best of my friends; wherefore, and from no other motive I think it my duty to advertise you that you are most particularly desired, to have especial attention to all he does, to show him all the respect imaginable, nor venture to say anything before him, that may either offend or displease him no in any sort; for I may truly say, there is man I love so much as M Compigne, none whom I should more regret to see neglected, as no one can be more worthy to be received and trusted in decent society. Base, therefore, would it be to injure him. And I well know, that as soon as you are made sensible of his virtues, and shall become acquainted with him you will love him as I do; and then you will thank me for this advice. The assurance I entertain of your Courtesy obliges me to desist from urging of this matter to you further, or saying any thing more on this subject. Believe me, sir, &c.   Richelieu

TESSA, SIMONE
AND FRIENDS

I wonder whether it was a keen anagrammatist at the Treasury who devised the acronym TESSA (Tax Exempt Special Savings Account) with an eye to the fact that this investment opportunity was an anagram of 'asset'.

I wonder whether any parents who name their children Simone do so in the hope that their little ones will benefit one day from the acquisition of 'monies'.

Many of our first names are anagrams of words as two dozen of those for boys and girls reveal:

GIRLS' NAMES

airman	Marian or Marina	**hurt**	Ruth
amble	Mabel	**ideal**	Delia
army	Mary or Myra	**label**	Bella
breath	Bertha	**osier**	Rosie
coral	Carol	**riding**	Ingrid
daily	Lydia	**road**	Dora
dean	Edna	**sets**	Tess
dine	Enid	**soar**	Rosa
fared	Freda	**sore**	Rose
gem	Meg	**teak**	Kate
goal	Olga	**threes**	Esther/Hester
great	Greta	**triads**	Astrid

BOYS' NAMES

brain	Brian		**lyric**	Cyril
cigar	Craig		**mail**	Liam
ducal	Claud		**meager**	Graeme
enters	Ernest		**nailed**	Daniel
events	Steven		**ordain**	Dorian
flared	Alfred		**rice**	Eric
glared	Gerald		**sinned**	Dennis
grade	Edgar		**smile**	Miles
ingle	Nigel		**spire**	Piers
lace	Alec		**vain**	Ivan
lark	Karl		**wander**	Andrew
line	Neil		**yonder**	Rodney

THE EYES HAVE IT –
THEY SEE

As you've no doubt spotted, 'the eyes' is a particularly apt anagram of 'they see'. Over the years there have been a few Countdown conundrums which have also had apt anagrams. For example:

dormitory	dirty room
ferocious	coo furies
headstone	one's death
magnified	find image
powdering	weird pong
streaking	great skin

Other conundrums have been derogatory, such as:

abolished	head boils
battering	bitter nag
emanating	mean giant
hardening	dinner hag
hastening	tennis hag
similarly	slimy liar

. . . while others have been simply serendipitous:

adaptable	a bald pate
butchered	Dutch beer
earnestly	nasty leer
episcopal	Pepsi Cola
fanatical	facial tan
frugality	fruity gal
scarecrow	soccer war
sploshing	long ships

You can get a lot of fun out of forming anagrams with appropriate (and sometimes telling) associations. Here are some more:

alphabetically	I play all the ABC
angered	enraged
astronomer	moon-starer
conversation	voices rant on
degradedness	greed's sad end
desperation	a rope ends it
disconsolate	is not solaced
endearment	tender name
lubrication	act – rub oil in
measurements	man uses meter
misrepresentation	interpret one amiss
mother-in-law	the warm lion
parishioner	I hire parson
pittance	a cent tip
point	on tip
predestination	I pertain to ends
presbyterian	best in prayer
punishment	nine thumps
revolution	love to ruin
saintliness	least in sins
schoolmaster	the classroom
separation	one is apart
soft-heartedness	often sheds tears
staghounds	a hunt's dogs
suggestion	it eggs us on
tempestuous	seems put out
uniformity	I form unity
upholsterers	restore plush
waitress	a stew, sir?

THINK POSITIVELY

When was the last time you felt 'consolate' or 'gruntled', or the weather was 'clement' giving you a feeling of 'gust'?

If your answer is a little time in coming, don't despair. All the words in quotation marks are more familiar when in their negative sense; their positive forms are seldom, if ever, used.

Here are some more that change with the power of positive thinking:

antibiotic	biotic (relating to life)
deodorant	odorant (something odorous)
disinfectant	infectant (something that infects)
feckless	feckful (efficient, powerful)
illicit	licit (legal, allowable)
immaculate	maculate (marked and untidy)
impeccable	peccable (inclined to sin)
impervious	pervious (something capable of being penetrated)
indelible	delible (able to be deleted)
indomitable	domitable (capable of being tamed)
ineffable	effable (able to be uttered or expressed)
inevitable	evitable (avoidable)
innocuous	nocuous (harmful)
insipid	sipid (tasty, full of flavour)
uncanny	canny (familiar, without mystery)
unconscionable	conscionable (scrupulous, conscientious)
uncouth	couth (polished, polite)
unkempt	kempt (tidy, trim)
unspeakable	speakable (capable of being spoken)
unwieldy	wieldy (manageable)

TIME AFTER TIME

For well over half a century Time magazine has been peppering the English language with new words, a good many of which have worked their way into everyday use, Time popularized 'beatnik', 'tycoon', 'pundit' and 'Sinologist'. If cinemactor, cinemactress and cinemogul didn't catch on, plenty of other words did. Here are some which have all come into being since Time first hit the news-stands:

amorific	horsepersons	radicalesbians
anti-opera	jivernacular	roadies
anti-star	lumpengrandiosity	schleprechaun
apocalypticians	mailgrams	sci-fireworks
audioanimatronically	Maocidal	sexscraper
Beatledammerung	mathemagician	sociohysteric
bewilderness	mazemania	space-bopper
biographoid	megabuckers	superbug
blaxploitation	megadisaster	supercrooner
buffdom	Msapprehension	superpregnancy
Californicated	Msogamy	superscapegoat
Carterphobia	occultivated	systemaniac
cavepersons	oligosyllabic	televangelist
chillout	orgasmatron	UFOria
counterklutzical	outcumbent	underworldly
crediholics	paperkrieg	unsavvy
cultercats	parafictions	urbanscape
Disneyfication	petroglitter	verballistics
eco-activists	petropolitics	vestphobe
ejaculatorium	phallocrat	watch-birds
girlcott	philodendrophiles	womandarin
growthmania	plantochondriacs	wommanequin
heightism	polycopulative	womlibby
hippophile	prognosticide	

TOM SWIFTIES

Tom Swifties are a type of pun based on adverbs or adverbial phrases. They take their name from a character in a series of books by Edward Statemeyer, published in the 1920s and they work like this:

'Turn on the radio', said Tom with a short wave.

'How about a game of draughts?' asked Tom airily.

'I'll try to dig up a couple of friends,' said Tom gravely.

'I got the first three wrong,' said Tom forthrightly.

'Drei . . . fünf,' said Tom fearlessly.

'Let's trap that sick bird,' said Tom illegally.

'That's a very large herring,' said Tom superficially.

'Pass the cards', said Tom ideally.

'And lose a few', said Tom winsomely.

'The bacon is burnt', said Tom with panache.

'I like to go camping,' said Tom intently.

'Drop that gun!' said Tom disarmingly.

'I bequeath,' said Tom willingly.

'Brothers,' said Tom grimly.

'I can't find the apples,' said Tom fruitlessly.

'I've just had a serious operation,' said Tom half-heartedly.

'Xs and,' said Tom wisely.

'Zero', said Tom naughtily.

'Coda,' said Tom finally.

TWO'S COMPANY

If you're a Scrabble player, like Mark Nyman (*Countdown's* own World Scrabble Champion), you'll appreciate the value of the two-letter words you're allowed to play in the game. I'm pleased that *Countdown* contestants are never stuck with two-letter words, but if any of them ever had the bad luck to be in that position, a list like this could come in very useful.

As the founder of the British Scrabble Championships, Gyles Brandreth has made a study of unusual and, in scrabble terms, invaluable words, of which these two dozen are selection:

aa	a type of volcanic lava	**ka**	a personality double
ai	a South American sloth	**ki**	any of several Asian and Pacific trees
bo	a variant of 'boo'		
ch	south-west dialect form of 'I'	**li**	a Chinese unit of measure
da	a heavy Burmese knife	**ob**	an objection
di	plural of *deus* – 'god'	**od**	a force
ea	a stream	**oe**	a whirlwind
ee	Scots form of 'eye'	**om**	a mantra
fa	a musical note in tonic solfa	**oo**	an extinct Hawaiian bird
fy	an interjection	**ug**	a feeling of disgust
gi	a costume for judo or karate	**yi**	in Chinese philosophy, the faithful performance of one's specific duties to society
gu	a kind of violin played in the Shetland Isles		
io	a large Hawaiian hawk	**zo**	a type of Asian cattle
jo	a sweetheart		

U AND NON-U

Earlier we had a look at words beginning with Q without being followed by the customary U and here is a selection of words that contain Q without being followed by U. The one exception, and there's always an exception, is zaqqum, the only word I've come across in the language that manages to have it both ways with a U and non-U Q.

bathqol	a divine revelation in Hebrew tradition
burqa	a veiled garment worn by Muslim women
cinq	the number five in dice or cards
cinqfoil	any of several plants of the genus *Potentilla*
coq	a trimming of cock feathers on a woman's hat
faqih	a Muslim theologian versed in Islamic religious law
faqir	a Muslim ascetic
fiqh	Muslim jurisprudence based on theology
fuqaha	plural of 'faqih'
Iraqi	a resident of Iraq
miqra	Hebrew text of the Bible
muqaddam	a headman
nastaliq	Arabic script used principally in Persian verse
paq	a large rodent of Central and South America
pontacq	a still wine from the South of France, red or white
sambuq	a small Arab boat
shoq	an East Indian tree
shurqee	a south-easterly wind that blows in the Persian Gulf
suq	a marketplace in the Muslim world
taluq	an Indian estate including subtenants
taluqdar	a collector of a taluq's taxes
taqlid	the uncritical acceptance of Muslim orthodoxy
tariqa	the Sufi path of spiritual development
trinq	a toast, used in Rebelais's *Pantagruel*
waqf	a charitable trust in Muslim law

yaqona	an intoxicating beverage made from the crushed root of an Australasian shrubby pepper
zaqqum	a tree with bitter fruit, mentioned in the Koran
zindiq	a heretic showing extreme infidelity to Islam

UGH!

My attention was drawn to 'ugh' by an entry in the magazine *Logophile* a few years ago. This quoted Charles C Bombaugh's 1905 book *Facts and Fancies for the Curious* in which he presented the reader with a passage intended to point up 'the absurdity of that Indian grunt in our language, "ugh".'

This is what Bombaugh's readers were faced with ninety years ago. How easy do you find it to read aloud?

Hugh Gough, of Boroughbridge, was a rough soldier on furlough but a man of doughty deeds in war, though before he fought for this country he was a thorough dough-faced ploughman, his horse having been houghed in an engagement with the enemy. Hugh was taken prisoner and, I ought to add, was kept on a short enough clough of food, and suffered from drought as well as from hunger. Having, on his return home, drank too large a draught of usquebaugh, he became intoxicated, and was laughing, coughing, and hiccoughing by a trough, against which he sought to steady himself. There he was accosted by another rough, who showed him a chough near, also the slough of a snake, which he held at the end of a tough bough of eugh-tree, and which his shaggy shough had found and had brought to him from the entrance to a sough which ran through and drained a slough that was close to a lough in the neighbourhood.

130

UNIVOCALICS UNITE

Whereas a lipogram concentrates on omitting a particular vowel, a univocalic is the exact opposite; restricting itself to the sole use of a particular vowel.

For this reason univocalic verse presents a remarkable, if somewhat contrived, cohesion.

This Victorian univocalic about the Russo-Turkish war relies on A as its only vowel;

> War harms all ranks, all arts, all crafts appal;
> At Mars' harsh blast, arch, rampant, altar fall!
> Ah! hard as adamant a braggart Czar
> Arms vassal-swarms, and fans a fatal war!
> Rampant at that bad call, a Vandal band
> Harass, and harm, and ransack Wallach-land.
> A Tartar phalanx Balkan's scarp hath past,
> And Allah's standard falls, alas! at last.

The turn-of-the-century author Charles C Bombaugh composed univocalics for each vowel. Here is 'The Approach of Evening' which he wrote for the letter I:

> Idling, I sit in this mild twilight dim,
> Whilst birds, in wild, swift vigils, circling skim.
> Light winds in sighing sink, till, rising bright,
> Night's Virgin Pilgrim swims in vivid light!

The univocalic is by no means the preserve of the nineteenth century. Slightly less than thirty years ago, George Marvill composed this for a competition in the *New Statesman*. Look carefully and you'll see that he succeeds on two accounts. Not only is O the only vowel used, his exchange between the owls is a palindrome!

> 'Too hot to hoot!'
> 'Too hot to woo!'
> 'Too wot?'
> 'Too hot to hoot!'
> 'To woo!'
> 'Too wot?'
> 'To hoot! Too hot to hoot!'

VALENTINE RHYME

'Valentine Rhyme' is one of the creations of that world-beating punster Alan F G Lewis. It's one of the brilliantly crafted puns he calls Terse Verse. Here it is with a selection of his other classics:

Valentine Rhyme

My heart and I
Call to you
But you're too deaf
To Eros

The Tree of Love

Yew witch Hazel
It's plane
I'm sycamore poplar girls
And aspen alder time
On the beech
And pine to cedar day
When I maple to say
'Hazel lime yours,
Cumquat may.'

Please Be Seated

When she said 'Howdah do
Take a pew
You look divan'
I thought 'This is sit'
But I was throne aside
When she decided to settle
For a puffe.
A sort of plinth charming
Who promised to support her
For the rest of her dais,
Next time I'll be more chairy.

I Told Her

I told her no sensible man
would take her dancing
in her bikini.
So she went
with a little moron.

VICE VERSA

A word that can have two opposite meanings might seem to be of limited value and therefore seldom used, so it's interesting to discover that quite a few commonly used words have diametrically opposed meanings. Some of the definitions may not be familiar, but they can all be found in larger dictionaries, notably Webster's.

bent	crooked/levelled
bless	sanctify/curse
dust	remove dust/add dust
fill	pour in/pour out
help	aid/hinder
infatuate	inspire/frustrate
let	allow/hinder
overlook	inspect/neglect
rout	rummage out/assemble
shend	destroy/protect
sit	remain seated/stand
square	agree/differ
stand	remain upright/lie flat
sweat	produce moisture/dry thoroughly
take	receive/give
thrill	titillate/bore
tickle	touch lightly/beat
trim	embellish/remove
trip	move nimbly/stumble
weather	wear well/wear out

VOX POP

William Shakespeare may have used 22,000 words in the course of his writing career but most of us get by with not many more than 2,000 in day-to-day speech. Of those the top dozen are;

1 the	**4** to	**7** that	**10** it
2 of	**5** a	**8** is	**11** for
3 and	**6** in	**9** I	**12** as

According to Stuart Berg Flexner, the author of I *Hear America Talking*, two words 'I' and 'you' represent ten per cent of all 'informal conversation'. He lists (in no particular order) the rest of the top fifty spoken words as;

the	will	for
he	don't	out
it	are	over
they	can	about
him	go	just
them	say	that
an	see	is
to	tell	was
in	a	have
with	she	do
from	we	want
and	me	would
now	her	think
not	what	be
this	on	know
get	of	thing

WAS IT A RAT I SAW

As I have already mentioned. there is something very satisfying about letter patterns. They can also present quite a challenge intellectually when you start to analyse them. Take the palindromic sentence WAS IT A RAT I SAW, pleasingly arranged like this. How many different ways are there of spelling out WAS IT A RAT I SAW by starting at any of the Ws and passing from one letter to an adjacent one? (Answer on page 160).

```
               W
             W A W
           W A S A W
         W A S I S A W
       W A S I T I S A W
     W A S I T A T I S A W
   W A S I T A R A T I S A W
     W A S I T A T I S A W
       W A S I T I S A W
         W A S I S A W
           W A S A W
             W A W
               W
```

WORDSEARCH

The popular party game Charades doubles as an equally successful word puzzle. Clues are supplied for the separate syllables of a word, 'my first', 'my second', etc and then for the complete word 'my whole'. Armed with this information, the solver then has to work out the identity of the mystery word.

Try your deductive powers on these classic Charades before checking the answers on page 160.

A Royal Residence

My *first* is near the dear bright sea,
The green waves oft it lave;
It glitters in the sunshine
Lies in the deep dark cave.
My *second* is quite endless,
Like the love of which it tells,
A bright idealization
Of Love's eternal spells.
My *third*, alas! to say the truth,
Suggests a vacant sty.
My *whole*, a royal residence;
Now, prithee, tell me why.

Fruit

Some at my *first* will catch,
But not upon the thatch.
The sexton does my *second*,
His labour it is reckoned.

My *whole* is most delicious,
When summer is propitious.

In the fields

The fields are golden in the sun;
The breezes make a rustle
As o'er the nodding ears they run;
And lo! with merry bustle,

With tawny skins, and sickles keen:
The reapers come a-trooping;
And see, my *first* around is seen,
With heavy tops down-drooping.

The mill's tall sails are spinning round,
The breezes blow them gaily;
With store of grain the stone is crowned
And does its labours daily.
The air is white with misty meal,
Before the task's conclusion;
And hoppers, heaped full high, reveal
My *second's* soft profusion.

A handful, see, of ripened wheat,
I'm in a bunch combining;
The poppy red, the woodruff sweet,
Among the ears entwining:
And – prettiest bloom that ever grew
In cornfield, dale or dingle –
My *whole,* whose hue is heaven's own blue,
Shall 'mid the wheat-ears mingle.

Ride On, Ride On

Ride on, ride on, thou traveller bold,
And cast thy looks on *first*:
See how the tempest clouds do lower,
That soon in storm shall burst.
Ride on, ride on, thy *second* leads
Across the lonely heath,
Where gibbets tell of darksome deeds,
And culprits swing beneath.
Ride on, ride on, my *third* thou art,
An honest one and true:
Beware! a *third* is lurking near,
Who would his hand imbrue.
Ride on, ride on, ride for thy life,
Spur on thy faithful steed,
For now my *whole* thy *second* bars,
Nerved for his lawless deed.

XENAGOGUE TO X

A 'xenagogue', in case you didn't know, is a guide and here it is guiding you through some of the lesser known words that begin with the letter 'x'.

'Xylophone' and 'X-ray' are two of the most familiar X words, but larger dictionaries like Webster's, are rich in others that get less of an airing. Here are some of them:

xanorphica	a stringed musical instrument
xanthocyanopsy	colour blindness in which the ability to distinguish only yellow and blue is present, vision for red being wanting
xanthoderm	a person with yellow skin
xebec	a Mediterranean sailing ship
xenia	gifts sometimes given compulsorily to medieval rulers and churches
xenodogheinonology	the lore of hotels and inns
xeriff	a gold coin used in the Ottoman Empire
xerophagy	the eating of dry food
xerosis	abnormal dryness of the skin
xilinous	of cotton
xiphoid	sword-shaped
xoanon	primitive image carved in wood
xu	a monetary unit of Vietnam
xurel	a fish
xylantrax	charcoal
xyloglyphy	artistic wood carving
xyomancy	divination through the use of piece of wood
xylopolist	a timber merchant
xylosistron	a musical instrument
xystus	a walk lined with trees

YOU GO URUGUAY, AND I'LL GO MINE!

We have Groucho Marx to thank for the title – and the script of *Animal Crackers*.

Groucho was a master of the pun. 'Did you ever meet a fellow named Jonah?' he asked a Welsh woman. 'He lived in Wales for a while.' In *Cocoanuts* he remarked, 'What's a thousand dollars? Mere chicken feed. A poultry matter.' And in the same film he shared a truly awful pun with Chico:

GROUCHO: We're going to have an auction.

CHICO: I came over here on the Atlantic auction.

Puns on place names are particular favourites of mine. To pursue the North Atlantic Drift, Franklin Pierce Adams had this to say about Christopher Columbus:

> Oh, I should like to see Columbus's birthplace,
> And then I'd write a fine, authentic poem,
> And critics, none of whom would read it through,
> Would say, 'At least we have the Genoan article.'

Turning to present-day upheavals, the Californian earthquake inspired the idea of establishing a San Andreas Fund, which just confirms that some Americans can be generous to a fault.

Still in California there's the lament that Hollywood's eternal triangles invariably end up as wreck tangles. And down in the south you'll get the advice that you can always tell a baby from Alabama because it has a southern drool.

Puns aren't for everyone. As the saying goes, 'One man's Mede is another man's Persian', but they help raise a smile when the real world isn't much to laugh about:

How did you catch that plane from Teheran?
Iran!

The situation in the Gulf isn't improving – things are going from Iraq to ruin.

At least no one will go hungry in the Middle East because of all the sand wich is there.

Puns help us in foreign countries and unfamiliar cultures:

In Athens: Even if the Greeks invented the deep frieze, they didn't think it was worth Parthenon.

In Moscow: It must have been the vodka Russian to my head that made me see red.

In La Paz: I'll take your word for it, but will the police Bolivia?

In Santiago: I wouldn't mention human rights unless you want a Chile reception.

In Kenya: How are you enjoying your holiday? Safari, so good.

In Paris: Soupçon is French for a small amount, only morceau.

In Berlin: Schnapps and hock are my favourite Teutonics.

Perhaps we'd better slip away at this stage. As somebody put it:

Absinthe makes the tart grow fonder

and as someone else wisely remarked:

She told me he was just a travelling companion, but I sensed arrival.

Y Oh! Y

The letter Y is often overlooked as a vowel because it is generally regarded as a consonant. As a written variant of I , Y acts as the sole vowel in many words which would have no vowels at all if Y wasn't there – words like:

by	lynx	sly
cry	my	slyly
crypt	myrrh	spy
cyst	myth	sty
dry	nymph	sylph
fly	ply	thy
fry	pry	try
gym	pygmy	tryst
gypsy	rhythm	why
hymn	shy	wry
lymph	shyly	wryly
lynch	sky	wych

YOU NAME IT

'What's in a name?' asks Shakespeare's Juliet, 'That which we call a rose/By any other name would smell as sweet.' Though if 'rose' began with a capital letter, making it the forename 'Rose' the same might not necessarily be true.

What's in a name, then? The answer in many cases is a word in its own right. I'm not aware of a 'richard' but a 'carol' is something everyone enjoys singing at Christmas and there are plenty of similar cases when forenames can drop their capital letters and slip into a different identity. So here's a sort of *Who's Who* of a selection of name/nouns and their definitions:

Abigail	a lady's maid
Albert	a short watch chain
Anna	a coin once used in the Indian subcontinent
Basil	a herb
Beryl	a precious stone
Bill	a bird's beak
Bob	up and down motion
Cicely	the name of several plants
Clement	mild
Clementine	a type of orange
Dick	a detective
Dicky	a false shirtfront
Dolly	a trolley used for film and television cameras
Don	to put on
Faith	reliance, trust
Flora	plants of a region or epoch
Frank	open, candid
Grace	short thanksgiving at mealtimes
Harry	to harass

Iris	part of the eye
Ivy	climbing evergreen plant
Jack	device for lifting weights from below
Jean	twilled cotton fabric
Jenny	female bird or animal (especially a female donkey)
Jess	short strap round the legs of a hawk
Joey	a young kangaroo
Ken	to know
Martin	a bird
Matt	without lustre
Nelly	large sea bird, the giant petrel
Nick	to steal
Olive	evergreen tree with oily fruit
Patty	a little pie or pastry
Peter	to fade away
Rob	to steal
Robin	small brown red-breasted bird
Rosemary	a fragrant shrub
Ruby	a precious stone
Ruth	compassion, pity
Sally	to rush out suddenly
Ted	to turn over and spread grass for drying
Terry	a pile fabric
Victor	a winner

ZAPPA AND ZAPPA

Moon Unit Zappa and Dweezle Zappa were two of the more remarkable residents of Hollywood, a neighbourhood not unfamiliar with the exotic and bizarre.

The Zappas are not alone in having a name that sets them apart from the rest of the human race. If you want to be one of the crowd be a Chang. Estimates vary but there are considerably in excess of 100 million Changs on earth. If you want to stand out in the crowd you'll need to have a name as unusual as these, all of which have been borne at some time by otherwise ordinary people:

Mark Clark Van Ark, who lived/s in Toledo, Texas

B Brooklyn Bridge, who had a policy with the John Hancock Life Insurance Company

Reverend Christian Church, who was active in the Italian city of Florence

Groaner Digger, an undertaker from Houston, Texas

DeFred Go Folts, a university administrator at Harvard University

Lettice Goedebed, of Johannesburg, South Africa

T Hee, who worked in a restaurant in New York City

Rapid Integration, who featured in *Newsweek* magazine

Judge Judge, who administered justice in Pasadena, California

Moon Bong Kang, a Korean diplomat

Buncha Love, who also came to the attention of *Newsweek*

A Moron, who occupied the position of Commissioner of Education for the Virgin Islands

Santiago Nudelman, who worked as a publisher in Brazil

Violet Organ, an art historian in New York City

Luscious Pea, a citizen of New Orleans, Louisiana

Rosebud Rosenbloom, who was enrolled at the Ethical Culture School in New York City

Cardinal Sin, the Archbishop of Manila

Justin Tune, chorister from the class of 1947, Westminster Choir, Princeton, New Jersey

Peninnah Swingle Hogencamp Umbach, a spiritualist minister from Charleston, South Carolina

Mr Vroom, a motorcycle dealer from Port Elizabeth, South Africa

Gisella Werberserch-Piffel, another Hollywood resident, an actress this time

ZIKR, ZLOTY AND ZWIEBACK

English dictionaries aren't rich with words beginning with Z but *Webster's Third New International Dictionary* lists a good many imported words from other languages, three of which are 'zikr', 'zloty' and 'zwieback'. These are also three of the most unusual words now used in English and as a concluding section on our remarkable language what could be better than a glimpse of some of the other less familiar of its estimated 490,000 words (not to mention its 300,000 technical terms).

axolotl	a salamander
bdelloid	like a leech
crwth	an early Celtic musical instrument
ctetology	a branch of biology
dghaisa	a type of small boat found in Malta
djebel	a North African hill
dukw	an amphibious vehicle
dzeren	a species of gazelle found in Asia
fremd	unrelated
gmelinite	a mineral
hamscon	burglary
hjelmite	a mineral
iao	an Australian bird
ioa	a seabird found in the tropics
iynx	a woodpecker
jheel	a pool, lake or marsh in India
kvass	a type of beer
kokerboom	the quiver tree
kyoodle	to yap
mbori	a disease in camels

ngege	an African fish, important as a source of food
nsambaya	an African tree
ouabaio	another tree, from southern Africa
qutb	an Islamic saint
sdrucciola	a musical term
squdge	ooze
sravaka	a direct disciple of Buddha
tjaele	frozen ground
tmesis	the separation of the parts of a compound word
tzut	a head covering consisting of a brightly patterned square of cotton
uang	a Brazilian tree
vly	a temporary lake
voeu	a proposal
yclept	named
yperite	mustard gas
zikr	a ritual formula
zloty	Polish monetary unit
zwieback	a sweetened bread

ANSWERS

ANSWERS TO ABRACADABRA
on page 7

There are 1,024 ways to spell ABRACADABRA.

ANSWER TO QUEEN VICTORIA'S ACROSTIC
on page 24

The town is Newcastle famous for coalmines:

A city in Italy	NapleS
A river in Germany	ElbE
A town in the United States	WashingtoN
A town in North America	CincinnatI
A town in Holland	AmsterdaM
The Turkish name of Constantinople	StambouL
A town in Bothnia	TorneA
A city in Greece	LepantO
A circle on the globe	EcliptiC

ANSWER TO BOXING CLEVER
on page 25

You can solve the puzzle in twenty-three moves – the fewest possible.
Move the squares in this order: A, B, F, E, C, A, B, F, E, C, A, B, D, H, G,
A, B, D, H, G, D, E, F.

ANSWERS TO C PLUS
on page 27

ARK	RACK	CRACK
HAT	CHAT	CATCH
HATE	CHEAT	CACHET
HEAD	ACHED	CACHED
HERE	CHEER	CRECHE
IRK	RICK	CRICK
LEAN	LANCE	CANCEL
LOUT	CLOUT	OCCULT

NEAR	CRANE	CANCER
NEAT	ENACT	ACCENT
NOSE	SCONE	SCONCE
OAST	COAST	ACCOST
OIL	COIL	COLIC
OUST	SCOUT	STUCCO
RILE	RELIC	CIRCLE
ROSE	SCORE	SOCCER
SEAR	SCARE	SCARCE
SOUR	SCOUR	CROCUS
SPITE	SEPTIC	SCEPTIC
TAPE	EXPACT	ACCEPT

ANSWERS TO CRYPTARITHMETIC
on page 32

1
```
      5
      5
      5  +
     15
```

2
```
      9
     89  +
     98
```

3
```
   9567
   1085  +
  10652
```

4
```
    850
    850
  29786  +
  31486
```

5
```
    106              104
  19722     or     19722
  82524  +         82526  +
 102352           102352
```

ANSWERS TO DICTIONARY WITH A DIFFERENCE
on page 36

1 *Raising Arizona*
2 *North to Alaska*
3 *Blue Hawaii*
4 *California Suite*
5 *Paris, Texas*
6 *Oklahoma!*
7 *New York, New York*
8 *The Kentucky Fried Movie*
9 *Nevada Smith*
10 *The Great Northfield, Minnesota Raid*

ANSWERS TO DOUBLE RIDDLES
on page 41

1 The two answers are: LETTUCE and SPINACH.

2 The two answers are: BERMUDA and ICELAND.

ANSWERS TO FROM HEAD TO TAIL
on page 53

1		2		3	
P I G		F O U R		W H E A T	
w i g		f o u l		c h e a t	
w a g		f o o l		c h e a p	
w a y		f o o t		c h e e p	
s a y		f o r t		c r e e p	
S T Y		f o r e		c r e e d	
		f i r e		B R E A D	
		F I V E			

4		5		6	
P E N		N O S E		T E A R S	
e e n		n o t e		s e a r s	
e e l		c o t e		s t a r s	
e l l		c o r e		s t a r e	
i l l		c o r n		s t a l e	
i l k		c o i n		s t i l e	
I N K		C H I N		S M I L E	

```
7  W E T          8  H A R E         9  P I T C H
   b e t             h a r k            p i n c h
   b e y             h a c k            w i n c h
   d e y             s a c k            w e n c h
   D R Y             s o c k            t e n c h
                     s o a k            t e n t h
                     s o a p            T E N T S
                     S O U P

10  E Y E         11  P I T Y        12  S T E A L
    d y e             p i t s            s t e e l
    d i e             p i n s            s t e e r
    d i d             f i n s            s h e e r
    L I D             f i n d            s h i e r
                      f o n d            s h i e s
                      f o o d            s h i n s
                      G O O D            c h i n s
                                         C O I N S

13   E E L         14  P O O R        15  R A V E N
     e e n             b o o r            r i v e n
     p e n             b o o k            r i s e n
     p i n             r o c k            r i s e r
     P I E             r i c k            M I S E R
                       R I C H

16  O A T          17  T R E E       18  G R A S S
    r a t              f r e e            c r a s s
    r o t              f l e e            c r e s s
    r o e              f l e d            t r e s s
    R Y E              f e e d            t r e e s
                       w e e d            f r e e s
                       w e l d            f r e e d
                       w o l d            g r e e d
                       W O O D            G R E E N

19   A P E         20  C A I N       21  F L O U R
     a r e             c h i n            f l o o r
     e r e             s h i n            f l o o d
     e r r             s p i n            b l o o d
     e a r             s p u n            b r o o d
     m a r             s p u d            b r o a d
     M A N             s p e d            B R E A D
                       a p e d
                       a b e d
                       A B E L
```

```
22  T E A       23  C O M B      24  R O G U E
    s e a           c o m e          v o g u e
    s e t           h o m e          v a g u e
    s o t           h o l e          v a l u e
    H O T           h a l e          v a l v e
                    h a l l          h a l v e
                    h a i l          h e l v e
                    H A I R          h e a v e
                                     l e a v e
                                     l e a s e
                                     l e a s t
                                     B E A S T
```

ANSWERS TO LETTER LINE
on page 79

1 Strengths
2 Rhythms
3 Defencelessness
4 Boldface, feedback
5 Misrepresentation, representationism
6 Uncopyrightable, misconjugatedly
7 Strengthlessness
8 Overnervousness
9 Indivisibility
10 Bookkeeper

ANSWERS TO MAP REFERENCE
on page 83

1 Chad, Andorra
2 Bermuda, Nepal
3 Iran, Vietnam
4 Tonga, Togo
5 Gabon, Mali
6 Peru, Uganda
7 Poland, Denmark
8 Panama, Spain

ANSWERS TO MEASURING UP
on page 84

angstrom	one hundred-millionth of a centimetre
becquerel	radiation activity
cable	240 yards
coulomb	electric charge
farad	electric capacitance
gray	radiation absorbed dose
henry	inductance
hertz	frequency
jeroboam	4 bottles of champagne
joule	work, energy, quantity of heat
kelvin	thermodynamic temperature
link	7.92 inches
mole	amount of substance containing as many elementary entities as there are atoms in 0.012kg of carbon-12
nebuchadnezzar	20 bottles of champagne
newton	force
ohm	electric resistance
pascal	pressure, stress
peck	2 gallons
quire	24 sheets of paper
radian	plane angle between radii of a circle
siemens	electric conductance
tesla	magnetic flux density
tun	216 gallons
weber	magnetic flux

ANSWER TO ONE AND ONLY
on page 92

ANSWER TO PUNCTUATION PLEASE
on page 100

That that is, is; that that is not, is not; is not that it? It is!

ANSWERS TO READ ME A REBUS
on page 103

1 It's a frame up

2 It's a square meal

3 It's six of one and half-a-dozen of another

4 It's a bad spell of weather

5 It's a bone (*b* on *e*)

6 *Much Ado About Nothing*

ANSWERS TO RIDDLES AND RHYMES
on page 108

1 A tree
2 Teeth
3 A candle
4 Rain
5 The letter R
6 Sunshine
7 A frog
8 A potato
9 A sawmill
10 A squirrel

ANSWER TO WAS IT A RAT I SAW
on page 137

You can spell WAS IT A RAT I SAW 63,504 ways!

ANSWERS TO WORDSEARCH
on page 138

A Royal Residence

Sandringham (Sand, Ring, Ham)

Fruit

Strawberry (Straw, Bury)

In the Fields

Cornflour (Corn, Flower)

Ride On, Ride On

Highwayman (High, Way, Man)